Finding Faith

Other books by Naomi Reed

My Seventh Monsoon
No Ordinary View
Heading Home
The Plum Tree in the Desert

For more information, please go to www.naomireed.info
www.facebook.com/myseventhmonsoon

Finding Faith

Inspiring conversion stories from around the world

Naomi Reed

Authentic

First published 2018 by Authentic Media Limited,
PO Box 6326, Bletchley, Milton Keynes, MK1 9GG
and Authentic Media Limited, PO Box 28,
West Ryde NSW 2114, Australia
authenticmedia.co.uk

British Library Cataloguing in Publication Data
A catalogue record for this book is available from the British Library.

ISBN: 978-1-78078-462-5
978-1-78078-463-2 (e-book)

Some names have been changed to protect identities.

Cover design by Junnifer Baya
Printed and bound in Great Britain by Bell and Bain, Glasgow

Copyright Acknowledgments

Contents

Come to me, all you who are weary and burdened,
and I will give you rest.

Matthew 11:28

Introduction

In early 2017, my publisher sent me an email. 'We have an idea for a new book,' they said. 'Do you have time to talk?'

'Yes,' I replied fairly quickly, 'I do have time to talk. I love ideas for new books!'

Later that week we spoke on the phone. The idea was to write a book that would tell the stories of a wide range of people who had come to faith in Jesus, later in life, and mostly out of other religions or world views. The key to the book, they said, would be the variety of the stories from around the world, and the focus on the way God is at work in individual lives, one by one. They wanted it to be an encouragement for all of us.

I was immediately interested. I love hearing stories of the way God is at work around the world! As we talked, I began to jot down ideas of people that might be interested in the project. My publisher also had some ideas for stories to include. Wouldn't it be amazing, I thought, if I could find some sort of pattern – some way that God tends to work as he draws people to himself? Or perhaps there would be a common question that people sit with, prior to understanding the gospel and the saving work of the Lord Jesus Christ. Or maybe a startling description of change and transformation in a country that I have never heard of. The possibilities were endless. So I began. I made a list of questions and I set off in search of the stories.

1

You are not alone

Michael – Iran and India

I began with Michael. He and his wife are currently living in a capital city in Australia; however, Michael grew up in Iran, and he studied in India. Mutual friends suggested that I meet him. 'He has a really good story,' they said. 'He grew up as a Muslim in Iran, and then he became a believer in India, through listening to Christian radio.' Fair enough, I thought. That sounds good. So I met Michael at a coffee shop near a train station, in the capital city. It was a bright, sunshiny day outside. We ordered drinks and sat down. The first thing he told me was that there was so much about his life that he couldn't tell me, or that he couldn't tell anyone. Michael's family is still in Iran. He himself has been in Australia for twenty-six years and he shares his life and faith openly now, but carefully.

Back in the 1960s, said Michael, Iran was a good place to grow up. His father was in the army, so their family moved around a lot, but they were always comfortable. Michael said that he himself was born in Ahvaz, in the south of Iran, and then grew up in Isfahan, where the family lived in a house with a large garden and lots of fruit trees. The children were always playing soccer outside, or *biaoboro*, a form of cricket. When Michael was 13, they moved north to the capital city, Tehran.

'My parents were nominal Muslims,' he said. 'They didn't attend the mosque regularly because, as Shi-ites, attendance wasn't compulsory and they could pray at home. My father would occasionally open the Quran and read it out loud to the family in Arabic. When I was in primary school, I studied the Quran as part of the primary school curriculum. I remember sitting in class and practising correct pronunciation for every word and sentence. If we didn't do it correctly, it would be sinful. But the meaning of the words was not explained to us – it was reading and memorising that was important, not understanding. Then when I was in high school, I studied Arabic, mainly from stories and poems, because the Arabic used in the Quran was too hard to understand. It was classical.'

'Do you remember praying, as a child?' I asked.

'Yes,' he said. 'It was compulsory, at school. I went to a private school from year 1 to 3. There was no prayer in public schools but, at my school, everybody would be lined up, kneeling in a row, with our hands washed . . . and the leader would stand in front of us, reciting prayers, by rote, always without mistake. We listened. But I only prayed at home when I needed to, when required, or before exams. For me, belief in Islam was never enforced, but I did believe in it, sometimes out of fear, and sometimes because I wanted to get something good out of it. I thought that if I did good things, I would get what I wanted.'

'And Ramadan?'

'Everybody celebrated Ramadan,' smiled Michael. 'Even if we didn't fast during the day, we still celebrated in the evenings. I remember the sweets – *zoolbia* and *bamieh,* in particular – special kinds of Persian doughnuts. The dough is deep-fried and then soaked in a saffron sauce. We'd eat really large naan with meat stew. Rice was expensive then. And someone would have to go and kill the chicken. But that was when I was in primary school, a long time before the Iranian revolution. After the revolution, if you didn't fast during Ramadan, you would be punished. If you ate in public during Ramadan, the revolutionary guards could arrest you. Or if you were a shopkeeper and you had food available, uncovered, the same thing could happen. You could be arrested and go to jail.'

'Did you have questions about God?' I asked.

'Yes,' he said, 'I did, but I was told not to ask them, because I could lose my faith.' Then he paused. 'I was mostly thinking about eternity. In our language that means the end. But I wanted to know about the beginning, about the time before creation. What was it like then? The Muslim faith talks about Adam and Eve, but it says nothing about the time before Adam, and I wanted to know what it was like when there was nothing. So I used to close my eyes and go back in time, in my mind. Sometimes I would worry that I'd go too far back in time and never be able to return.'

'Were you ever afraid?'

'No, I wasn't afraid of God. I thought God was good. But we were all afraid of the jinns, the bad spirits. We wouldn't want to go out at night, or anywhere where it was dark, because that's where the jinns were.'

'Had you heard of Jesus back then?'

'Yes, we had. We thought Jesus was a special prophet – one of the five special prophets in Islam. Altogether, there are 124,000 prophets in Islam and five of them are special – Noah, Abraham, Moses, Jesus and Muhammad. Muhammad is the final messenger and prophet. So I thought that Jesus was a good prophet. He did good things. I didn't know anything else about him. I didn't know that he died and rose again.'

In 1975 Michael finished high school and left for military training in a town one hour away from Tehran. While he was there, he also trained as a sports coach and he was sent to a village to teach sport. Through all that time, though, Michael's main aim was to leave Iran. He explained that it was becoming more difficult to live there and he wanted to experience other places. Also, Michael's friend had recently emigrated to the US, and Michael wanted to join him. Unfortunately, by then it was 1978, the middle of the Iranian revolution, and the US closed its borders to Iranian citizens. In Iran the Pahlavi dynasty was overthrown and later replaced by the Islamic Republic, under Ayatollah Khomeini. Michael couldn't go to the US. At about the same time, another friend told Michael that if he learned English before he went to the US, he would spend less money once he got there. So Michael went to India to learn English, and he still planned on going to the US, if he could.

In India, Michael said, he travelled to Chandigarh, in the northern Punjab state. It was a new, modern city, 260 kilometres north of New Delhi, and the city itself was very well organised, with the streets running in parallel. Michael enrolled in and studied for a Bachelor of Arts degree at the Chandigarh University, majoring in economics, English and Persian. 'It was very hard, though,' he said. 'I found it very hot and we only had water in the taps in the early mornings and for a few hours in the evening. Then I ran out of money.'

Michael explained that in the beginning the exchange rate between Iran and India had been good – the Iranian currency was strong. But then the Iran-Iraq war began and Iran needed all its funds within the country, so the government put restrictions on how much money their citizens could send out of the country. Michael soon realised that he needed to be very careful with money, only buying bread and vegetables when necessary. 'Later,' he said, 'I started asking my parents to send me goods instead of money. I could sell the goods in India, and buy food with the profit. So they sent me pistachio nuts – 5 and 10 kilogram bags. I sold the pistachio nuts and it worked well for a while, until the Iranian government put restrictions on the amount of goods that citizens could send out of the country. Then, my parents only sent me one 3 kilogram bag of pistachio nuts, once a year. The money didn't last long.'

After three years, though, he said that he completed his BA, and decided to move south to the city of Kurukshetra, in the state of Haryana, closer to Delhi, to study his Masters in linguistics. It was the only course available to him at the time, and he knew that he needed to keep studying in order to stay in India. He certainly didn't want to go back to Iran, especially during the war, and with the changes in the country, post-revolution.

'The religious leaders back in Iran seemed to be against everything,' he explained. 'They were against television. At the time, the television was in black and white and had nothing on it . . . but they were against it. I started to wonder why Muslims fought so much against themselves, and against others. The war between Iran and Iraq went on for eight years, and India was mostly peaceful back then. Before I lived in India, I had been told that only Muslims were good people. But in India, I had friends who were Hindus and Sikhs and Christians. I knew them all. I played soccer with them all, and I was the captain of the college team. That meant that lots of people knew me . . . and they were all my friends. So I started asking more questions. As Muslims, why are we fighting so much? Can we ever do enough good to outweigh the wrong? Can any of us? Can I? Usually, if I did something wrong, I tried to do something good. I gave money to the poor. It's called *zakat* – the third pillar of Islam, and a duty. But I would never give *zakat* to non-Muslims. I wouldn't want to help the infidel.'

It was while studying his Masters in linguistics that everything changed for Michael. One day in 1984, Michael got a letter from a friend who was living in another state of India. The friend was also from Iran and had become a Christian. The letter explained how it had happened. The friend had also been a nominal Muslim, like Michael. Michael read the letter and was not very interested. He wrote back to his friend and asked questions, but only to increase his knowledge, generally. He didn't want to become a Christian.

'At the time,' Michael explained, 'I didn't realise that the Christian and Muslim views were so different. We had heard of Jesus as a prophet. In Persian poetry, Jesus is spoken of highly. But then after a while, I started to listen to Christian radio, mainly because the station also played Hindi music, from the Hindi films, which I liked. And there were a couple of Christian programmes being broadcast at the time. One of them was called *Back to the Bible*.'

One day, Michael said, he heard the broadcaster offer listeners a correspondence course if they wanted to know more about the Bible. Michael wrote to the programme and asked for the material, because he wanted to increase his knowledge generally. He didn't want to become a Christian. He remembers the day he received the booklets. He read one in particular. It was about the character of God. It said that God was unchangeable, omniscient, omnipresent, just, merciful, compassionate . . .

Michael smiled. 'As Muslims,' he said, 'we were discouraged from talking about God. We never talked about what he was like, or about his character or attributes. Now, by myself, in India, I was reading about God, about his character. All I wanted to do was to read more.'

In the city of Kurukshetra at the time – 1984 – there were no public churches and no Christian bookshops. But somehow, Michael found a King James Version of the Bible and he began reading it from the beginning. 'I only read three chapters of Genesis,' he said. 'And I decided that the Bible was logical. In the Bible it says the devil became the devil because he wanted to be like God, and that made sense to me. In the Quran, the devil became the devil because he didn't bow down to Adam, which doesn't make sense to me. In the Bible, Adam and Eve were in the garden, which also makes sense to me. In the Quran, they were in heaven, which doesn't make sense to me because there could be no sin there. The Bible seemed logical from the beginning.'

But then after Genesis, Michael started on the New Testament. 'That's when it happened,' he said. 'I read the Gospels and I just fell in love with Jesus.' Michael smiled, remembering. 'I saw that Jesus was someone who practised what he told other people to do. I'd never seen that before. I didn't know anyone else who did that. I loved him. There was no fault with him, at all. In John 14:6, it says that Jesus said to his disciples, "I am the way . . . the truth and the life. No one comes to the Father except through me." And I knew if Jesus is a prophet, and prophets never lie, then Jesus must be the only way to God, so I kept reading the Bible and I came to John 8:31,32, where Jesus said, "If you hold to my teaching, you are really my disciples. Then you will know the truth, and the truth will set you free." And that's exactly what happened to me, in that moment. The truth set me free. I became a Christian. I just knew. I believed in Jesus. I prayed to God in that city of Kurukshetra. I kept praying.'

At the time, Michael explained, there were no public churches, so he found a house church, and he met with other Indian Christians and was later baptised. Sometime afterwards, he moved to Delhi. He remembers praying to God and asking for help, talking to him all the time, and going to all-night prayer meetings and seeing answers to prayer. He began to read more of the Bible and he understood that salvation was by faith in Jesus and the grace of God, not by the good things he could do, or not do . . . and that a relationship with God was like nothing he had ever experienced before.

'What did your parents think?' I asked.

'Well,' said Michael, 'I was sure I had found the truth, and I assumed that other people, including my parents, would be happy for me. I hadn't heard of any other stories of trouble. So the following year, at the end of 1985, I decided to go back to Iran to tell my family.'

Before Michael left India, he told a friend that he might need a Christian contact in Iran. The friend in India passed on the need to a friend in the UK. The friend in the UK knew of an Assemblies of God (AOG) church in Tehran, and passed on the information to Michael, saying that the church held worship in his language, Farsi. Some weeks later, Michael arrived in Tehran, and he visited the church. In those days, the government did not want Muslims going inside churches, or potentially converting. Michael went inside and once he was inside, he saw a few hundred Armenian Christians, as well as some Muslim-background believers. It was the first time Michael had heard the gospel in Farsi. He was given a Farsi Bible. 'It changed me,' he said. 'Sometimes, in English, it's hard to read and I forget it. But in Farsi, I found I could remember it. I wanted to share it in Farsi. I *wanted* to explain it.'

Back at Michael's family home, though, it was not easy. That night, Michael told his parents and siblings that he loved Jesus. They were not happy at all. His father immediately worried about their reputation, saying, 'What will people think of us? Who will want to marry your sisters? What will they say about us? They will say that we have not brought up our family well. We will have a bad name.'

There was an argument. Michael went out to the front courtyard area, where he often slept. 'But I couldn't sleep,' he said. 'I was distressed and crying. I complained to Jesus. I wanted to know why he'd sent me here on my own. In the Gospels, he sent his disciples out two by two, and there I was on my own and I didn't understand it.

But just then, as I was complaining and crying, I saw Jesus. It wasn't a dream. I saw Jesus standing there. He was a man in light, walking towards me. I could not see his face but he took me by the hand. Then Jesus said to me, "You are not alone. I am with you, always, until the end of the age." And then I stopped crying.'

Michael told me how comforted he felt. It was amazing – he wasn't alone! He continued to pray, and he spent time with his family, but he also knew that it would be difficult to be a believer in Iran. So after three months, Michael decided to return to India. But there was a problem with that. If anyone had seen him at the AOG church, or spied on him reading the Bible, he might not be allowed to leave Iran. There were consequences for leaving the Muslim faith. Three days before he was due to fly to India, Michael was asked to submit his passport to the authorities, as part of normal practice. In most cases, travellers got their passports back on the day that they flew, if they were permitted to leave. But Michael was worried that he might not be allowed to fly. He had written his Muslim name on the form he had to fill out. Then there was a question. 'What is your religion?' Michael had stopped. If he wrote 'Muslim', it would be a lie. If he wrote 'Christian', he would be in trouble and would not be allowed to leave the country. It would be obvious to the authorities that he had converted from Islam. So he prayed for guidance. He didn't know what to do. He left the question blank. He didn't answer it.

Three days later, at the airport, Michael received his passport back and he was allowed to leave Iran. He said he didn't fully relax until the plane was in the air.

Michael explained that, back in India, he got a scholarship to do his PhD in linguistics at Kurukshetra University and, at the same time, he applied to the UNHCR and received refugee status. At first, the authorities didn't believe that he was a Christian. What if he was claiming persecution to get a visa? So Michael produced all the Bible correspondence course literature that he had completed in India, and he asked the man in the office, 'Do you think anyone would waste their time reading all of this if they didn't believe it?' The authorities took the material, looked at the extent of it, and agreed with him.

Receiving refugee status meant that Michael didn't have to go back to Iran. However, he did have to keep applying for refugee status every six months, to stay in India. After his PhD, Michael worked for the UNHCR, teaching English to refugees, and then he worked with Operation Mobilisation (OM), with Iranians and Afghans in India. It was going well but, by 1990, Michael realised that he couldn't stay long-term in India. It was very difficult to keep reapplying for refugee status every six months. So at the end of that year, Michael applied for a visa to Australia as an Iranian refugee. He was accepted and arrived in Australia in 1991.

At this point in the story Michael paused and asked me whether I'd like to walk to their church nearby, where Michael now pastors a Farsi congregation. I said that I would. It was mid-week and almost lunchtime. The street was busy. Inside their church hall it was also busy – it was full of whiteboards and coffee urns and chairs and about sixty Iranians and Afghans, all sitting down, learning English as a second language. As we walked in, Michael's wife was pouring the coffee. She looked up and greeted us.

'We've been at this church for nearly thirteen years, now,' Michael explained. 'And it's growing. It's one of a growing number of Farsi churches in this city in Australia. We have about a hundred people every Sunday. They come from every part of the city and we run TESOL[1] classes through the week. Sometimes up to 150 people come to the English classes, when there are lots of refugees. Many of them have come to Australia by boat. On Sundays they like to hear the Bible in their own language. They love to sing, especially fast, happy songs, with lots of clapping, so if we don't have a musician, we sing anyway. And we share about Jesus.'

'When you share Jesus with Iranians and Afghans, where do you begin?' I asked.

'I always start with Genesis,' said Michael. 'I always start with the story in the garden. We have all sinned, I say. And if salvation was by good works, God would have told Adam and Eve to do good works, to stay in the garden and do lots of good works to repair it. But he didn't. He banished them. So salvation is not by good works. I think, in the back of our minds, we all know that we can't do enough good works. Who would decide how much good works we need to do? And how can we do enough? We can't. We need forgiveness. I do. We all do. That's why God sent his Son, Jesus. And a Muslim needs to recognise who Jesus really is – his character, and that he is God himself. Jesus has saved us. But Iranian Muslims can be very difficult to reach. Evangelism can be very hard and discipleship can be even harder. But the important thing is to know them and to love them, to be friends with them, to be wise about where to start, to find out what is his or her real need or question . . . because everybody has a real need or a real question.'

I agreed with Michael, and then he showed me a video of their congregation singing and clapping, as well as baptisms and weddings and other celebrations. He pointed out the children in the video who had recently come to Australia by boat. Michael's wife finished pouring coffee and she came over to say hello, joining the conversation, and offering cheese and grapes. She explained to me that she and Michael met while he was in India, and they married twenty-four years ago, not long after he arrived in Australia. They now live near the church, and their two sons are at university. They are both busy pastorally, and in the future Michael would love to have more time to write – especially Bible commentaries for Iranians, in Farsi, and devotions for Christian radio in Iran.

'Would you ever go back to Iran?' I asked.

'We would love to,' they both said. 'Our sons have never been to Iran and they don't really know their grandparents. They have met them once, but naturally they can't develop a deeper relationship.'

'But Michael can't go back,' said his wife. 'If he was a nominal Christian, it might be OK, but he is a pastor and he is known to be a pastor. Recently we heard of two other Iranian Christians who went back and they were both detained. One of them is still in jail and we don't know what happened to the other one. In Tehran, the AOG church in Farsi has been closed down. The bishop was murdered. The remaining believers are being spied on. It's very difficult.'

I listened to her and began to understand why Michael couldn't tell me the rest of his story. Apparently, Michael's family members think that he is teaching at a university in Australia.

'What keeps you going when it's hard?' I asked.

Michael paused. 'I'd give anything to follow Jesus,' he said. 'When I saw him that time in our front courtyard, I knew that he loved me. It started like that. He loved me. Then he called me. And he told me that he'd be with me, always. So now if I'm having troubles in my ministry, or if I'm missing my home in Iran, I just remember that Jesus has called me, and he has told me, "I am with you, always, until the end of the age." And back in the Gospel of Matthew, when Jesus said that to his disciples, the context was mission. Jesus said he'd be with his disciples as he *sent* them, to the ends of the earth. It's the same for us, today. Sometimes it will be very difficult, for all of us, I know, and it has been difficult for me. It is difficult back in Iran, but every day Jesus is with us. That's what keeps me going.'

I had one last question: 'How are your parents, now, today?'

'They're OK,' said Michael, smiling. 'My father has been listening to Christian radio.'

2

What about the holocaust?

Judith – Austria and Uganda

My husband, Darren, and I currently attend a lovely church in the Blue Mountains, west of Sydney. We really enjoy the warm welcome, the fresh ways of looking at God's truth, and the honest conversations with people who agree that life is hard sometimes, and that Jesus changes everything. One day a new couple arrived at our church, and they sat next to us. We greeted them and we introduced ourselves. Their names were Judith and Clive. After we greeted them, the service continued and everything was going well, except that during that particular evening, one of our pastors told a story from Nazi Germany to illustrate his biblical point. The story itself was about Hans and Sophie Scholl, a brother and sister team who distributed literature as part of the Christian German resistance movement during the Second World War. Hans and Sophie were both apparently committed Christians, and they were horrified by Nazi war crimes. In 1943, they were arrested by the Gestapo and later executed, at the ages of 24 and 21. Sophie is recorded as saying, on the day of her execution, 'How can we expect righteousness to prevail when there is hardly anyone willing to give himself up individually to a righteous cause?'

It was a sobering story, for all of us. We sat there listening, and wondering about our own lives, and our own calling to righteousness, in Australia. But next to us, the new couple seemed quite moved by the story, especially Judith. I thought she may have been crying. I wanted to find out more.

So, three weeks later, Darren and I invited Judith and Clive to our house for a meal. It was a lovely, relaxed evening. We sat on our back verandah and we ate chicken curry together and we shared parts of our stories. Judith explained that she grew up in Vienna, Austria, with a Jewish father and a Catholic mother. Both her grandparents on her father's side were survivors of the holocaust, and two-thirds of her extended family died in the Nazi concentration camps. Judith herself became a Christian in her thirties, while working in Uganda, where she also met Clive. Judith and Clive had settled in Australia ten years before.

'What did you think of God, growing up in Austria?' I asked.

'I thought that God was there,' said Judith, 'but he was cold and distant, and he expected perfection. In my mind, it was a bit like God had us all on a retractable dog leash. He had given us each about 10 metres of leash and that leash was our conscience. It was like God said to us, "Here you go, here's your leash, and your conscience, so go and do the right thing, and in the end you will be judged for it." But we don't all use our 10-metre leash very well.' Judith paused and smiled. 'I don't. And back then, God was very hard to please. I couldn't please him. But as well as that, I had questions. Why does God allow suffering? What about the holocaust? What about the Jews? Did he look away?'

Both Judith's grandmother and grandfather on her father's side were Jews. Her grandfather originally moved to Vienna from Budapest and, at the same time, her grandmother moved there from Prague. They met and married in 1937. At around that time, there were two types of Jews in Austria – the wealthy, earlier immigrants who had moved there in the late 1880s and then the second wave – the poorer Jews, who had flooded the cities looking for work during the industrial revolution. In the 1930s, though, everyone was struggling financially, and the Jews became the reason, or the scapegoats. On 12 March 1938, Hitler annexed Austria to Germany (the Anschluss). He marched in with his armed forces and he began to carry out his anti-Semitic policies . . . and the vast majority of the Austrian people welcomed it. Jewish academic staff and doctors and lawyers were fired. Many of them tried to leave the country. Judith's grandfather and grandmother also tried to leave, but they were unable to get papers, and they were immediately targeted. They were both social democrats and their neighbours denounced them. Judith's grandfather was arrested straight away, and he was imprisoned for parts of the war. When he wasn't in prison, he worked for the resistance. Judith's grandmother went into hiding for the entirety of the war, and their family home was taken over by the Nazis.

'My father was born in 1946,' explained Judith, 'immediately after the war. But his elder brother was born in January 1938, two months before the Anschluss, so he was also in hiding, as a little boy. Then sometime in 1940, my grandmother gave birth to a baby girl. Not long after that, the Gestapo knocked at the door of their hiding place. The baby started to cry and my grandmother tried to settle her, and to muffle the sounds of her crying. My grandmother held a blanket to the baby's face and the baby died, accidentally smothered by the blanket.'

Judith looked up, with tears in her eyes. 'Sometimes people in Australia seem interested in the war, or they're even obsessed by it. Perhaps they know someone who fought in it, or they've read books about it . . . but to me they seem distant from it. For me, it's my *story*, my family, my heritage. My grandmother never recovered. She always had fear in her eyes. Afterwards my grandfather kept working for the resistance movement. They both managed a hotel as a respite place for the trade unions, and they were always scared.'

Judith explained that her father grew up in the midst of this and, for a period of time, the family even stopped practising as Jews. They were too worried by then, too fearful of further persecution. Even as recently as the 1990s in Austria, said Judith, there was a political move to the right and Austria became the first European nation to have a leader from the far right back in government. His name was Jörg Haider. It was still possible, said Judith, that even then, anti-Semitism had not died out. People in his party even denied the existence of gas chambers. Could anyone blame Judith's family for being fearful?

But mostly, Judith remembers her father's questions. He had unending questions. He wanted to know why the Catholics didn't stand up for the Jews during the war. Back then, Austria was about 85 per cent Catholic. The question for so many of the Jews was . . . why didn't the Catholics do anything? If they believed in God, why didn't they question the holocaust? Why did they look away? And if there was (or is) a good God, why did he allow it? Why did so many of his followers do nothing? For Judith's father, the questions were personal and he would often rant. 'Six million Jews!' he would say. 'How could God allow it? Who would allow suffering like that? Did God look away?'

Judith remembers asking the same questions herself during her teen years. She still has the gold necklace that her grandmother wore in hiding during the war. There are teeth marks on it, where her grandmother bit into the gold, terrified. But as well as that, Judith remembers celebrating the Jewish Passover with her wider family, and lighting the Hanukkah candles, and listening to her uncle explain the Passover to all the children present, in Hebrew and in German. For a short time, Judith and her brother Markus also went to a Jewish youth group. It was good to be able to celebrate their heritage and to understand who they were, but Judith explained that she and Markus were also not fully accepted. The other kids said, 'Your mother is a *goi*,' which was a disparaging name for a non-believer.

Judith's mother went to the local Catholic church, and so Judith also spent part of her childhood attending that church. Occasionally they would make pilgrimages to a basilica dedicated to Mary. Judith remembers the candles and gingerbread and the best nativity scenes in the northern hemisphere. But she also began to link her Catholic understanding to tradition. If she kept the traditions, she thought, and did good things, she would get material rewards, like gingerbread. Perhaps that's where the sense of a 10-metre leash came from. 'Although, at Easter,' Judith admitted, 'I remember we went to the Catholic church for the midnight service. Back then, we lived in the village of Reichenau, which is at the foot of the last peak of the Alps in Austria. It was surrounded by mountains and there were crosses on the mountains. We would go to the church in the dark and then the priest would walk into the building, carrying a candle. He would say that the light of the world had risen. Then we would all receive a candle and light our candles from his. Gradually, the church would become lighter and lighter . . . and then outside, the crosses on the mountains would be set on fire. "Jesus has overcome the cross," they would say.' Judith paused, 'Of course, back then,' she said, 'I didn't get it at all. I didn't understand the cross or the light. I just knew it was somehow powerful. I kept asking my questions and I kept trying to be good. My questions were always about theodicy. If God is just and holy and good, then how does such misery and evil exist in the world? Why does God allow it?'

Even as a child, Judith had a strong sense of justice and compassion. The family would sit around the dinner table and discuss world events, often heatedly. It was the 1980s and the time of the hunger crisis in Ethiopia. Four hundred thousand people died of famine. At the same time, the iron curtain was in effect, separating Eastern Europe from its Western neighbours. Many of Judith's extended family were living on the other side of the curtain, in communist countries. Judith knew that she couldn't visit them and they were being spied on. Then, in 1989, the Berlin wall came down, and in 1991, the First Gulf War, operation Desert Storm, occurred in Iraq. At the dinner table in Judith's house, the debates became more heated. How could they be so well-off when others were not? And how could some nations be dumping food surplus in the ocean, to keep the prices high, while others were starving? Had God turned his face away, again?

At one point, Judith decided to become a lawyer, to try to help. But then she changed her mind. Justice and the law were not always the same thing. So then she decided to become an aid/development worker. That would be a help. But meanwhile, her father was still ranting, 'Six million Jews! How could God allow it? Who would allow suffering like that? Did God look away?'

At the same time, Judith was realising that her 10-metre leash was not very long. 'I was in a dilemma,' she said. 'I was at university by then and I knew that I was doing some stuff that was not good, or the will of God . . . but I argued my way out of it. I explained to God that our society had moved on in regards to slavery, so we had obviously moved on in regards to our thinking about pre-marital sex, for example. Lots of people were living together. I was living with my boyfriend. And as well as that,' she admitted, 'I was surfing my way through a whole variety of drugs, particularly marijuana. But I was also doing good things,' she said. 'My university thesis was on "The utopian concepts in the Middle Ages", so I was reading Isaiah as well as Greek mythology. That gave me good points. It solidified in my mind that I was in a good place. I had a good understanding of the Bible (I thought) and I felt some pride. So in my mind, I wasn't perfect, but I was OK . . . and I wasn't aware of any emptiness then.'

From 1992 to 2003, Judith studied her double major degree in German literature and language, and art history, at the University of Vienna. She finished her thesis on the concept of utopia. As well as that, she did a diploma in radio journalism, travelled to the UK, cared for her sick aunt, and worked for the Austrian Broadcasting Corporation. By 2003 Judith had graduated with her double degree, and a completed thesis, but she still had a desire to become an aid/development worker. It was time to do something about suffering.

At the end of 2003, Judith's best friend called her to say that HORIZONT3000, a Catholic aid agency, were looking for radio journalists in either Brazil or Uganda. Judith had always been interested in South America, but the job in Uganda looked far more challenging professionally, so she applied for the job there. This meant she left Austria in January 2004, suddenly finding herself in the dry, sub-Saharan town of Arua, 480 kilometres north-west of Kampala City. Judith remembers the paved road that led them across the Nile River into Arua, and then it stopped after the first bend. Everything beyond that became dirt and dust. Judith was a very long way from the Alps.

For her first year, she lived on the outskirts of the town, next to the Catholic bishop, and she worked for the Catholic community-based radio station. She also discovered that the habits she had picked up in her own country could easily be transferred to East Africa. By the end of that year, Judith was fired from her job for excessive partying.

'It left me a bit embittered with the Catholic Church,' she admitted. 'I held a grudge for a while. I thought there was so much hypocrisy within the church. I suppose I hadn't understood the difference between faith in God and religion as an institution. That was still to come. But during my time in Uganda, I made a lot of valuable connections and I quickly found a job as a consultant with the United Nations. I worked in Mozambique and Zambia with the UN, and then with the BBC in Tanzania.'

'Did you ever go to church in Africa?' I asked.

'Yes,' she said. 'During those years I would often visit African churches with my local colleagues. They would invite me to go with them and I would say yes, as a sign of respect. Sometimes, the service was in English, sometimes it was in the local language. But nothing particularly stood out to me.'

Then, in early June 2006, Judith went to work with a human rights project in Kitgum, northern Uganda. In that area, the Lord's Resistance Army (LRA) had held the country in civil war for decades. The Ugandan army had tried to fight back and, as a result, millions of Ugandan people were living in camps for Internally Displaced People. Each camp would consist of thousands of round African huts, with families squashed together in tiny spaces. At the time, the UNHCR described it as the worst refugee catastrophe of the world. Human rights violations in the camps were extreme – women were being raped, under-age people were being recruited to join the army, and domestic violence was rife. The idea of Judith's new work was to raise internal awareness of the situation through a media campaign.

For many of the people, the war had been going on for so long that they couldn't remember anything else. They needed to be told that they didn't have to put up with the violations. So the first thing that Judith did was to find a radio station that was well received within the camps and could partner with their project. Back then, of course, there wasn't electricity, television or the Internet, so radio was their best option for communication. It turned out that the best radio station within the camps was a Christian, charismatic radio station, attached to the first Christian City Church (C3) in Africa. A local man named David Livingstone was the pastor of the church and the manager of the radio station.

Judith began consulting with David regarding the human rights project and they immediately hit it off. She found out that David had been orphaned quite young and recruited by the LRA as a child soldier. He was later captured by the Ugandan army, and transferred to a prison in Kampala. But while he was in prison, someone who had known his grandfather recognised him, and they let him go. David was then adopted by a New Zealand missionary and he became a Christian, and later a pastor. In speaking to David, Judith was immediately impressed by his passion and commitment to his local community, even within civil war. David was not turning his face away from the horrors.

Soon after meeting each other, David introduced Judith to his wife and their three children. He also invited Judith to their local church in Kitgum and, of course, Judith went. She was in the habit of saying yes to church invitations! David's church was held in a brand-new building. There were not even windows yet. Inside, there were nearly eight hundred people. Judith had never seen anything like it. The people seemed happy. They were singing, loudly. Judith slipped into the crowd and tried to hide, but on that particular day, there were only about ten white people, so that made it difficult. Then, quite early in the service, David stood up at the front of the church and said, 'We have a friend called Judith with us today. She doesn't really know Jesus yet, but God has a plan for her and we're going to give her a Bible.'

Judith remembers walking through the crowd to the front of the church and receiving her Bible. It had a bright blue cover with silver pages. Judith sat back down in her seat. Then there was a guest preacher from Tanzania, who spoke about the Israelites in the wilderness. The preacher said that the Israelites were often looking back, scared of the unknown, and wanting the familiar. Then the preacher asked the congregation, 'Does anyone here feel like they're in the wilderness and the grass is greener everywhere else?' Judith had never been in a church where the preacher asked the congregation a question, and the people actually answered it. Half the congregation raised their hands. Then the preacher agreed with them. 'Yes,' he said. 'I often feel like I'm in the wilderness and I want to turn around.' Judith had never been in a church where the preacher actually admitted that the Christian walk could be hard sometimes. Then the preacher said, 'If you feel like turning around today, please come forward and we're going to pray for you.' All the people who had raised their hands earlier, flocked to the front of the church. Judith had also never been in a church where people actually responded like that. She remembers watching them and feeling envy.

'That's when it hit me,' she said. 'I became aware of a huge emptiness inside me. I realised I was envious because they knew a God who I had never encountered – a God who you could go to when you didn't have it all together, a God who you could talk to when you didn't have it all figured out. I had never imagined that. I thought that God had an unattainable standard – that he was cold and distant and I couldn't possibly get there, or please him. Now here he was, acutely personal, interested in my day-to-day. It just blew me away. The people around me seemed to actually know him. He was somebody you could encounter. I just felt a profound sense of emptiness and I started crying. I didn't mean to, or want to cry. It was embarrassing. But it felt like God opened the floodgates and I couldn't stop. There was so much pain being washed out. All around me, people started praying for me, and hugging me. I didn't even know them. They were complete strangers. They spoke in a language I didn't understand . . . and yet there was so much kindness.'

After the service, Judith was invited to go with the church members to a crusade on a local football field. There was another guest speaker and Judith remembers still crying. 'I knew something big was happening to me,' she said, 'but I didn't understand it. So afterwards, I went home and I tried to read some of the books that David had given me, but they didn't make any sense to me.'

Not long after that, the communications job in Kitgum came to an end, and Judith moved on to another project in another part of Uganda. But somehow, wherever she went, David seemed to keep popping up unexpectedly, in the unlikeliest of places. The final time occurred in Jinja. Jinja is a town not far from Uganda's capital, on the shores of Lake Victoria. Judith had a good friend living there and she went to visit her. Coincidentally, Jinja was also the town where David grew up with his adopted mother. David popped up again and asked Judith if she would like to come and meet his mother, Anne.

Judith went with David and she met Anne. As soon as they were introduced, Anne invited Judith to sit down with her on their front porch, and she began telling Judith her own story. It was strangely similar to Judith's. There were questions and pain and struggles that were very alike. As Anne spoke, there seemed to be no judgement in her voice, just an honest account of her story and a reminder of God's love.

'Somehow, it was like Anne knew what I'd been through,' said Judith. 'I don't know why or how she knew, but she did. She kept assuring me that God loved me. That was the second time I cried and I couldn't stop. I was overwhelmed by the truth that God actually knows me and pursues me. Anne sat with me on the porch for hours and she let me cry. David was somewhere in the distance. God kept saying, "Come as you are." I could just come. I didn't have to have the answers to my questions, or my act together. He was simply God and he wanted me to come.'

That evening, Judith and David went to pick up a Chinese takeaway. While they were waiting for the order, David asked her if she wanted to pray and commit her life to Jesus. Judith did. It was 1 July 2006 and, for the first time, Judith realised that she could stand before God. Jesus had taken away her sins and died for her. She was forgiven. She could come.

It changed everything. Judith started to read her Bible, and the literature. She had a million questions. She would often phone David and ask him them, one by one. David tried to answer the questions. Judith moved cities again, this time to Dar es Salaam. In Dar es Salaam, she didn't know of a church, or a Christian, so she kept reading the Bible by herself. At about that time, David put her in touch with an Australian Christian man who had previously visited Uganda. His name was Clive. Clive also tried to answer Judith's questions.

'But it was good,' smiled Judith. 'All I had was my Bible and the Holy Spirit, so early on I developed the discipline of reading and praying and letting God speak to me. I realised that he passionately desires to be in relationship with us. That's the most important thing. I had to respond. I started to make different choices about my behaviour. But they were my choices, out of love, not because I felt that I was on a leash.'

'And what about your questions about the holocaust?' I asked. 'Did you still think God looked away?'

'No,' said Judith. 'We're living in a fallen world.' She paused. 'And we're seeing a lot of fallenness, even now, everywhere. But I don't think that God is the author of evil. The Bible says that God cannot be tempted by evil and he doesn't tempt anyone.[1] It says that he is light and there is no darkness in him.[2] So, it's not like God is looking away, or not looking away. It's not even the question. There is so much evil and suffering that is man-made. And I think God weeps.'

'And the church?' I asked.

'In lots of ways, I wish that the church was more effective,' said Judith. 'But I've realised that I *am* the church. We all are. That's our responsibility today. We can ask ourselves, how would we respond in certain situations? Would we be like Hans and Sophie Scholl? I think we could be. We can have faith like theirs . . . because God's love for us is outrageous. And the only adequate response to God's outrageous love for us, is to have the same kind of outrageous love and compassion and courage, for the world. That's our calling. I would like to think that I'm an outrageous person . . .'

At this point in our meal and conversation, Judith looked at Clive, and he agreed with her. 'She is outrageous,' he said. Then Clive went on to explain to us his side of the story, his trips to Uganda, his meeting with Judith, his first impressions of her, and then their wedding ceremony in Austria, in 2007. David Livingstone apparently flew in from Uganda to Austria and performed their marriage ceremony there, in front of friends and family. Then, the same year, Clive and Judith moved to Australia, where Judith retrained as a trauma counsellor, and the couple later settled in the Blue Mountains, not very far from our local church. That's why we happened to sit next to them, the week that we were all wondering about Hans and Sophie Scholl, and our calling to righteousness . . . and that's why Judith cried.

By the time we had made sense of the story, our meal was finished, and we were in awe of God's work in the world, and his care for each of us, so personally. Clive and Darren began taking the plates inside, but I had a couple more questions for Judith.

'What would you say now, about God?' I asked.

'I would say that he is near,' said Judith, immediately, 'and he is not cold or distant. Nothing is too small for him to care about. He loves us. He's so close and he knows us so well. He pursues us. And there's no such thing as a retractable leash, at all. There was a lot of shame in my story, but God forgave me. That's the message of the cross. We cannot be good enough, and God sent Jesus to bear our punishment. It's a free gift. When we trust him, we are given a "not-guilty" verdict. It says in Revelation that at the end of the day, he will wipe away every tear. That's what I want people to know.'

'And for you, now, in Australia, are there still hard things?'

'Yes, there are,' said Judith. 'There are lots of hard things. I've recently been through a very difficult time. I can't tell you the whole story but I was assaulted. It's been an intense journey of pain and anger, but also of experiencing God in the depths of my despair, and ultimately, by his grace and his grace alone, letting go and forgiving. I don't know how people could ever come to terms with a trauma like that without the loving, healing arms of God around them. The truth is that his love and his grace are enough. Though I walk through the shadow of the valley of death I will fear no evil . . .[3] but forgiveness is a choice and it's often an ongoing thing. Deep hurts like that do not suddenly disappear, and as a counsellor, I wouldn't want to treat any kind of trauma flippantly. Forgiveness is a process and I keep deepening my understanding and revelation of it every day. It's an ongoing issue. But it's utter, daily dependence on God. I know I'm forgiven and loved, so I forgive. Even today, I know people in the Jewish community who have faced their perpetrators and forgiven them. God, in his grace and mercy, gives us his Holy Spirit, who points us in the right direction and enables us to serve him, out of love, outrageous love. It's the only answer to the question.'

'Thank you,' I said genuinely, to them both, and sometime later we all said goodbye at the front door – me still thinking about Judith's grandmother, and her baby girl, and the way that God pursues, and restores, and heals, over generations . . . because his love for us is outrageous, and because he wants us to come.

3

Why go back?

Rudra and Sara – Nepal

Darren and I first met Rudra and Sara in 2011, at an International Nepal Fellowship (INF) event in Sydney, Australia. They both grew up in a small Hindu village in central Nepal in the 1970s, and they moved to Australia in 1999. Darren and I also lived in Nepal for six years, so we connected with Rudra and Sara at that event, and afterwards we stayed in touch.

On one night in particular, Rudra and Sara invited us to their house in Sydney to eat *momos* with them. We went! *Momos* are one of our favourite Nepali dishes and Sara is a wonderful cook – steamed dumplings filled with spicy meat and served with an especially spicy *achar*. We tried not to eat too many of them and, in between mouthfuls, we asked them both about growing up in the village of Karkineta, Nepal. They explained that back in the 1970s the village had no electricity and the only form of transport was by foot. The road had not gone through yet. Rudra said that he was the eldest son of the village Hindu priest and Sara was the youngest daughter of the tea-shop owner. Neither of them owned a pair of shoes until they were 16. They both lived in mud houses with grass roofs and they ate meat once a year. Rudra said that his one goal in life was to leave the village as soon as he possibly could. Sara said that her goal in life was to appease the gods, and survive.

'My parents are Newari,' said Sara, 'That means they are from the people group who were the original inhabitants of the Kathmandu

Valley. Over time the Newari people spread to other districts in Nepal and my family lived in Karkineta. That's west from Pokhara. Back then, the tourists needed to walk through Karkineta to get to the Annapurna Range and the trekking routes, so many of them stayed at our tea shop, and they slept in the room above the buffalo. That was good because they paid rupees to stay there. It also meant that when I was a child, I used to wake up at 5 a.m. and collect water from the tap in the village, or at the well in the jungle, and I filled up the *gargris* at home; then I would light the fire, because the tourists needed to have a shower; then I would cut the grass for the buffalo; then come home and wash the dishes, after the tourists had eaten breakfast; then I would do *puja* to the gods and go to school at 9.30 a.m.

'I didn't get changed for school because I didn't have any other clothes. Sometimes I didn't have anything for breakfast. After school I would go and collect more water for the tourists, so they could shower again, and then I would do the dishes again, and cut the grass again, or help in the fields – sometimes I would plant rice, or cut wheat. Then I would do the dishes again, after the tourists had eaten dinner and, at about 10.30 p.m., I would sit down to do my homework. We had no electricity then so we lit the kerosene lamp. In winter I had one shawl and no shoes. My feet would often be swollen and cracked.'

At this point we stopped the story and I said sorry, on behalf of every tourist, everywhere. Darren and I had done quite a bit of trekking in the Annapurna region, especially during our six years living in Nepal, and we had often taken showers, without really thinking about it. But Sara smiled and said, 'It's OK. We needed the income.' And then we continued with the story.

Sara explained to us that Newari people traditionally follow the Hindu religion, with a mix of Buddhist thought and their own customs thrown in as well. In her particular family, according to tradition, pre-adolescent girls 'marry' the *bael* fruit (wood apple), a symbol of the god Vishnu. They believe that if the girl's husband dies later in life, the girl will not become a widow, as she is already married to the god Vishnu. Sara did this at age 8 and then, at age 12, she had another ceremony known as *Bahra Chuyegu*. She explained that she was put inside a dark room for twelve days, completely alone, without light, and ceremonially married to the sun god Surya. During this time, Sara was not allowed to speak to anyone or leave the room or see daylight. She was provided with food.

'I think that's why I'm so scared of the dark now,' said Sara, 'and back then, there seemed to be so many gods, 30 million of them. I remember that my mum would pray in the corner of the house to all of them, every morning and every night. I knew that if I didn't do the right thing, the gods would be upset and bad things would happen to me. I was so scared, I tried to be good, but I was never sure if I was good enough. There didn't seem to be any hope.'

Rudra's family were from the Brahmin caste, the highest caste in Hinduism. Rudra's father was the local Hindu priest in Karkineta, and Rudra was his eldest son, so that meant that Rudra spent his childhood reading the Hindu scriptures in Sanskrit. If his father went away from the village, Rudra was called on to enact the ceremonies himself. He said that he knew the *Swasthani* and the *Satyanarayan* almost by heart and he would often perform the *Sraddya* – the funeral rites and ceremonies after someone had died – to help them cross the river and get to heaven.

'I remember that I was always fearful of the gods,' he said. 'Not everybody was fearful of them . . . but I was. I knew. I'd read the Hindu scriptures and I knew what would happen if I did bad things. I would be punished. The gods would punish me. I especially remember the story of a 7-year-old girl. She did wrong things and, one day, she didn't give a beggar any money, so she suffered her whole life. She was forced to marry a 70-year-old man. As a child I would often think about that story and feel scared of punishment . . . so I tried to be good, so that I wouldn't be punished.'

When Sara and Rudra were 14, they noticed each other at high school and at the tea shop. Rudra said that he would often come to visit the tea shop and ask the tourists for a pen. At the same time Sara was falling behind with her homework, so Rudra lent her his homework, secretly. He knew that he was not allowed to speak to

Sara openly because they were from different castes. But he liked her, so Rudra wrote a letter to Sara secretly and she replied, also secretly. They both knew the story about a couple in their village who had been banished forever because they married from different Hindu castes. Rudra and Sara didn't want to be banished from the village, so they didn't tell their parents. Then in 1989, when Rudra was 15, he left the village, walking 56 kilometres to Pokhara.

'I was so happy to be finally leaving the village,' said Rudra. 'And I knew that I didn't want to ever come back, even to visit. It was too hard to live in the village. We had no electricity, no roads, no transport, and everybody had to work so hard, even to eat rice.'

Once Rudra reached Pokhara, he said that he finished his schooling at the Prithvi Narayan Campus, studying English, maths and science. During science lessons he heard about the theory of evolution and, for the first time, he questioned his Hindu belief systems. Then he read more books and decided that his Hindu traditions were perhaps stories that people had made up. He took off his sacred thread and cut his *tupi*, his traditional tuft of hair. There were no gods, he decided, and there was no punishment for bad behaviour. The only thing to be careful of was the law of the land. 'In my mind,' said Rudra, 'all I wanted to do was to finish my study, get a good job and buy a house and a motorbike . . . and never go back to my village, ever again. So I finished my study, got a job, taught for a while, and then I left for the capital, Kathmandu. By then, Sara was already there. She called me to come.'

Back in Karkineta, things had not been going well for Sara's family. The road was built through from Pokhara to Baglung, and the tourists began getting on a bus and heading to the Annapurna Range directly, completely bypassing Karkineta. Hardly anybody slept above the buffalo anymore, or had hot showers, or ate rice in the kitchen. Sara's family's income disappeared. Her father started drinking *raksi*, the local rice wine. Then one day Sara's mother found out that Rudra had been writing letters to Sara, and her mother was so angry that she pulled Sara's hair and dragged her across the room. Not long after that Sara met an older male tourist who ran an expedition company.

The older male tourist told her that he had a permanent house in Kathmandu. Sara immediately asked him if she could return with him to Kathmandu and help him in the house. She wanted to finish her study in Kathmandu and she needed a job.

The older male tourist said yes. He would pay Sara. Sara's mother also said yes, making Sara lie about her age. Sara was only 16, but she must pretend to be 18. Sara's mother said that it was the only way to become rich. That same week Sara left Karkineta with the older male tourist and went to Kathmandu.

When Sara arrived in Kathmandu she met the man's wife, who seemed to take an immediate dislike to her. Instead of paying Sara 1,000 rupees a month, as promised, the man's wife gave Sara 800 rupees a month ($10), which was not enough to pay her college fees. Sara made breakfast for the couple, washed their clothes by hand, cleaned their house and then left for college at 9.30 a.m. After college she did their shopping, cooked their dinner, washed their pots and cleaned their house again. There was no time to study, and there was not enough money to buy food. One day Sara was so upset that she began to cry. She had written to Rudra but he hadn't replied. She had also asked her mother if she could return home to the village, but her mother said no, she must stay with the white man. So Sara cried to the gods. She told the gods that if Rudra got the letter and replied to her, then she would buy a whole bunch of incense, as an offering. The next week Rudra replied to Sara and he came to Kathmandu, for a visit. Sara was so happy to have her friend with her. She stopped crying. She bought the incense and offered it to the gods. Then Sara spent the night with Rudra and fell pregnant.

'I didn't even know how people fell pregnant,' said Sara. 'Nobody ever told me. They didn't ever talk about it. Then my tummy started getting bigger and somebody noticed and told me to go to the doctor. So I went to the doctor and she said that I was pregnant. But I really wanted to study. So the doctor said that I could have an abortion. But abortion was a crime. I could go to jail. What could I do? My friend said to go and see a nurse. I needed to borrow money to pay the doctor and the nurse. The nurse gave me a tablet to get rid of the baby, but it didn't work. Then the baby started moving. It was too late. I didn't want to live. I didn't want to die either. I told Rudra about the baby and he said, 'It's OK. Don't worry.' He came to Kathmandu straight away and we went to the temple, just the two of us. We were married there. We didn't know how to get married, we just told the gods we were married. It was 1992.'

After that, Sara and Rudra found a small room together in Kathmandu. Sara had to stop studying, but she continued to work for the white people until the day the baby was born. That day, she took one day off, and gave birth to a little girl. They named her Pabitra. She had lots of dark, curly hair. They took the baby home. But three days later something happened to Sara's leg and Sara was paralysed for three months.

'It was very difficult,' said Sara. 'I couldn't walk . . . I couldn't work. I was incontinent. Rudra had to carry me everywhere on his back. Our family rejected us because of the marriage. We had no money and not much to eat. Rudra started looking for cauliflowers in people's gardens, and then slowly, after three months, I started to get better and I went back to work for the white people. That was good for a while, but then our daughter became very sick. She was seven months old and she started rolling her eyes. After a week, we took her to the hospital. She had meningitis.'

Rudra and Sara said that Pabitra stayed in Bir Hospital, Kathmandu for nearly five months. Sara also stayed with her during that time and once again she had to give up her job. They had no money. The doctors did four operations on Pabitra's head, but she couldn't move. She was very swollen, and she couldn't sit by herself. When Pabitra was 18 months old, the doctors said they could do nothing more for her, so they sent her home . . . and Rudra, Sara and Pabitra went back to their room in Kathmandu.

'We couldn't pay the bills,' said Sara. 'We had nothing. I thought the gods were angry with us. I thought the reason our daughter was ill was because I had sinned, and because of my sin, we were being cursed. Our daughter was ill, and we had no money, and it was all because I had slept with Rudra before marriage. So I tried to tell the gods that I would give them a big sacrifice if our daughter got better – I would give them a goat or a buffalo. But it didn't work. Pabitra got worse. I wanted to know . . . why are the gods not listening to me? I made vows to them and they didn't hear me. I fasted every Friday to the goddess Santoshi Mata, who was meant to help the poor and the struggling people. I went to the temple every Saturday and I gave *puja* and sacrifices to all the gods, but it didn't work. I couldn't please the gods. Where was I lacking? I always wanted to know how to please them. Then our little girl died. She was four years old. It was 1996. And I thought it was all my fault.'

We paused in the story again. It was impossibly sad. Afterwards, Sara told us that they slowly recovered. Sara found work in an Indian garment factory. She cut the fabric into pieces and she earned forty-five paisa for each piece (half a cent). In one month, she made 200 rupees ($2.50). On top of that, she carried bricks and sand in a *doko* on her back, for a building project. Then Rudra began to learn typing and computing, and he started a small business selling carpets and Buddhist *thangkas*. The business began to do well. After a while Sara also found work for an American man and he paid her 1,800 rupees a month ($22.50). Not long after that, Rudra was offered work with the World Health Organization. He even went to Japan for a conference and he presented a session on women's health. Rudra and Sara were able to save money over the next few years and, in 1999, they came to Australia. It was what Rudra had always wanted. It was a very long way from their village of Karkineta.

'What was it like,' I asked, 'arriving in Australia?'

'When I arrived in Australia, I was so happy,' said Rudra. 'I had a telephone number for our relatives in Sydney, but they didn't respond straight away. So we took the bus to Central station and we found a backpacker hostel and stayed there for two days.'

'And sometime later,' said Sara, 'we met my cousin Yashoda. She lived in Liverpool [a suburb of Sydney], and after a while she invited us to come to her church. It sounds like a nice place, I thought. I had never heard of a church. I had never seen a Bible or heard of the Christian God, or the name of Jesus, so I went with Yashoda to her church. I walked into the building and I looked around me and there was no god anywhere. There were people singing. As soon as they started singing, I felt like I needed to cry. It was not sad crying, it was good crying. I had goosebumps over my arms. I had never had goosebumps before. I wanted to know why I was crying. I looked around me everywhere and I still couldn't see any gods. I wondered if my Hindu gods were angry with me because I was going to the white person's temple. Was that why I was crying?'

The next Sunday, Sara said that she had to work, so she couldn't go to church with her cousin. But the following week, she went to church again and the same thing happened. She noticed goosebumps on her arms and she started to cry. She felt a bit scared. What if the Hindu gods were angry with her? So, after church, Sara found a Hindu temple in the suburb of Minto and she went there with Rudra to do *puja* and to appease the gods. She thought that worked. She also fasted three times that week. But then her cousin Yashoda invited them to a 'house fellowship', and when Sara went inside, she saw people praying. 'I felt the same thing,' she said. 'It was something very strange in my heart, so I left the building and I went and sat outside. I didn't want to make the Hindu gods angry. After that, I stopped seeing my cousin, and I stopped going to church.'

Meanwhile, Rudra was not interested in church. 'We found jobs,' he said, 'and we found a place to live. We had two little boys. We had a barbecue in the garden. Life was good. We didn't need to go to church.'

Then in 2005, Rudra and Sara went to the birthday party of a friend's little boy. It happened to be held on a day that Sara was fasting to the god of death, Shani. Sara explained to us that Shani was a very dangerous god. 'We went to the Indian temple at Westmead that morning,' said Sara, 'to pray to the god Shani, and then we went to the birthday party in the afternoon. I didn't eat at the party, though. And after the birthday party, my friend invited us to a "combined fellowship" that evening. I said yes, OK, we would come. I remember sitting down at the fellowship. As soon as they started praying, I felt it again, the crying. So I said to Shani god, "I've been fasting, I don't want to cry, you have to save me." But the crying didn't stop and Shani didn't save me. I went to the toilet and a friend was there. She heard me crying. She said, "Why are you crying?" I told her. She said, "Jesus is calling you." I said, "Why would Jesus be calling me? We have 30 million gods." She said, "Jesus answers prayer and Jesus loves you."

'Afterwards, I went to church again, and that time I went down to the front and the pastor prayed for me. While he prayed, I felt something very warm inside me, and then I started to speak out loud. It went on for a long time. From that day on, I thought, "There is something very strong and very powerful in the Christian God." I'd never felt it before. I decided then that I would stop praying to the Hindu gods.'

Sara said that she went home that day and took down their religious lights and ornaments. She told Rudra that there was a big, strong God. Rudra didn't believe her at first, but Sara threw out their Hindu idols, and Rudra found them later in the bin. Sara felt like everything had changed. She had found the one true God and she slowly started to read the Bible.

'I remember reading the verse in Matthew 11,' said Sara. 'Jesus says, "Come to me, all you who are weary and burdened, and I will give you rest." I will carry you . . . Always before that, I had felt shame and fear, no assurance, no forgiveness, never fulfilled, always trying to please the gods. From then on, when I read that verse, I felt hope and assurance, because of Jesus, because Jesus said, "Come." The Hindu religion says that whoever does good things will be deemed righteous and whoever does bad things will be destroyed by the gods. I was always scared and worried about which god was angry. Then one day I read Romans 3:23. It says that we have *all* sinned, and that no one is good. Jesus died for us while we were still sinners. He loved us so much, he didn't look at our sin, he accepted us. He didn't wait for us to be perfect, he saved us while we were sinners, he gave us life.

'For the first time in my life, I felt hope and peace. I knew there was somebody to look after us and somebody who would listen to us. I knew that God would always do the right thing, in his time, for his plans and purposes, to grow us. It wouldn't always be easy, but I felt hope for the first time.'

In the meantime, Rudra had questions. He said he had started to go to church with Sara, but only because she wanted him to go. He didn't really want to be there, but he also didn't want to have an argument with Sara, so he went. 'I used to sit in church and work out how I could leave,' he said. 'Our boys would need to go to the bathroom, so I would take them out – even if they didn't ask to go. Then, while I was out, I would go next door to the Chinese shop, or to the bank. I stayed outside for as long as I could and I never listened to what the people inside were saying. I didn't like it. I wasn't interested. I especially didn't like the way they asked for money. For all that time, the only thing I was sure of was that I never wanted to go back to Nepal.'

At the beginning of 2011, Rudra and Sara said, they heard about INF – the Christian medical mission that had been working with the neediest people of Nepal since 1952. It had an office in Sydney and, coincidentally, INF was also the mission agency with which Darren and I worked in Nepal for six years. That same year in July, some of the people at Sara's church in Sydney invited Rudra and Sara to the annual INF event in Hornsby. They went.

'I went to the INF event because I had nothing else to do that day,' said Rudra. 'I remember that we sat down and there were speakers. They were Australians who had been working in Nepal for many years and they were back in Australia on home leave. They were telling their supporters about their work in Nepal. There was one couple in particular who had been living in Nepalgunj for many years. Nepalgunj is a really hot, difficult part of Nepal. It is down in the south. No one would want to live there. And that year, there had been terrible flooding. It was extremely difficult. The couple showed photos. Someone else showed a video of the surgery they were doing in Pokhara with the most disabled people in the country . . . people whom no one else would care for, people with leprosy.

'Then after that, there was an older Australian nurse who did a Skype call to us from Jumla. Jumla is in the far west. It's so remote. She talked about the new community health work in the most remote areas of western Nepal, and she laughed about the fleas and the bedbugs . . . She was covered in bites. But she was part of a work that helped the people who would otherwise die. It seemed that these Australians who lived in Nepal had been specialists back in Australia, doctors and health professionals. I'd been to see specialists in Australia . . . you have to wait three months before you can even see them . . . and they charge a lot of money! I just wanted to know why. Why would these specialists in Australia give up all of that and go to Nepal? They even had to raise their own money. They weren't paid anything. For me, I was born in Nepal, I knew the language, and I left the country when I was 25, saying that I would never go back. Why would these people go to Nepal?'

After the INF event finished, Rudra said that he went straight away to talk to one of the INF workers. He wanted to find out why . . . so he explained to the man that he had left Nepal twelve years earlier, and he could never imagine going back. He wanted to know, 'How could you go?' The INF worker said, 'Because the love of Christ compels me.' Rudra was amazed. He kept asking questions and they had a long conversation. The man said that the Bible tells us, as believers, that we respond to the love of Christ by sharing the good news and serving the neediest people of the world. Rudra was interested. At the end of the conversation, Rudra said that he would have a look at the Bible. He had never read it before and he didn't have his own copy, but he would borrow one from Sara.

Slowly, Rudra read the Bible, because of the stories at the INF day. At the same time as this, a group of Nepali Christians in Sydney began to set up their own church, run in the Nepali language, rather than attending services in English, as they had been doing. Rudra still didn't like the idea of church itself, but he liked the idea of a Nepali community, so he went along. And through all of that time, he kept thinking about the work of INF.

'Before I went to the INF event,' he said, 'I thought that people went to Nepal because it made them happy, like the tourists. I could understand that, but I couldn't understand why people would go to Nepal with INF, to serve the neediest people there, so I kept thinking about it. Then I read the Bible for myself and I realised that there really is a God and he cares for us, all of us. He's promised us eternal life through Jesus. I remember reading 1 John 1:9, "If we confess our sins, he is faithful and just and will forgive us our sins and purify us from all unrighteousness." I realised then that I needed to repent of my sins and God would forgive me. And I did. And he did. And he changed me.'

Since then, Rudra and Sara have grown in their faith and become a key part of the Nepali church in Sydney. Rudra has a role as the pastor and he often preaches on a Sunday. Many Nepalis have come to that church, especially those who are new to Australia. Sara now works locally as a nurse and Rudra runs his own business. Early on, Rudra began by purchasing a Red Rooster fast food shop near their home and he now owns multiple outlets, employing 330 people.

'It's what I always wanted,' Rudra admitted. 'I wanted to have money and a house to live in . . . and to never go back to Nepal again. But now I've changed. I don't even think about the money. I don't even think about how much I earn. The Bible says that we brought nothing into the world and we will take nothing when we go.[1] And that's true. So I trust God and I do what I can with my money. I love to go back to Nepal. I go back every year to my village in Karkineta. I support what INF does. We have fund-raising events all the time for the work of INF in Nepal. I lead vision trips to Nepal for INF and I help in every way I can. That's how I've changed! Also, we have good relationships with our family in Karkineta and some of them have become believers.' Rudra smiled. 'I try to share the love of Christ everywhere I go.'

'What would you want people to know, more than anything?' I asked.

'We don't need to despair,' said Sara. 'God loves us and he is in control. That's where we find true hope and peace.'

'God is so powerful,' said Rudra. 'He can do what he wants. And he reveals himself to us in different ways, and in different times. He doesn't always give us what we want. But he forgives us, because of Jesus. He changed me. He changed everything about me. It's true what that man said at the INF event . . . "The love of Christ compels me." Now it's the same for me. The love of Christ compels me. He makes me want to respond, with everything I have.'

We agreed with Rudra and Sara, and we thanked them for sharing their story, and for their generosity to us, and to their people, over so many years. The *momos* were particularly delicious that night, and as we mentioned that, Sara got up and went into the kitchen. She came back with a very large bag full of spare *momos* to take home for our sons.

4

Who can bring change like that?

Christy – Singapore

Christy was born in Singapore in 1975, and she has lived there for most of her life. She married Nan in 2002 and they have two small children. Darren and I happened to visit Singapore in April 2015. We were there primarily because Darren was speaking at a physiotherapy conference; however, we also spent time wandering around the colourful streets, taking photos of temples, admiring the city state of 5 million people, drinking dandelion tea, and sampling delicious, unknown Asian food at the markets. We even attended an inspiring Christian missions event, and it was there that we met Christy.

We liked her straight away. She was small, with dark hair, and she seemed to be always smiling. She was also the organiser of the event, which went very well, so afterwards we went out to a local restaurant to celebrate. We sat down and ordered a variety of *Zi Char*, and everything tasted better when we had someone to explain it to us! During the meal, I asked Christy about her faith background. She said that she grew up with a mother who was a staunch Buddhist-Taoist. Her family lived in a small public flat initially, and then, as her father's business grew, they moved into a two-storey house in central Singapore. In the living room there was an altar, quite prominently located. Every day, Christy would walk past the altar on her way to the dining room, or to her bedroom. She would burn incense at the altar. She believed in the spirit world. She respected the deity. On special occasions, the family offered the deity chicken, flowers and tea.

'Do most houses in Singapore have an altar?' I asked.

Christy explained that many Singaporeans say they come from a Buddhist background but, in pure Buddhism, they do not use altars, or worship statues. Pure Buddhism is philosophy. However, Buddhist-Taoism combines the two – philosophy and altars. More often than not, in Singapore, there is a mix of religions. Singapore is actually one of the most religiously diverse nations in the world, with most of the major religions coexisting relatively harmoniously. We nodded at that point, having noticed the mix of Buddhist and Hindu temples, as well as Muslim mosques. Christy then said that her family didn't actually participate in ancestral worship (involving urns filled with the ashes of deceased ancestors) at their house; however, they did participate at Christy's uncle's house, and they prayed daily to a deity for protection and peace.

'Praying to the deity was part of our family tradition,' explained Christy. 'Every day we would burn incense, mostly out of respect and fear. In Singapore there is a feeling of uncertainty about life and the future, so we would often go to the Buddhist temple and pray for protection, peace, health and wealth. We had a general idea of doing good, for the purpose of securing a place in heaven.'

'Is it hard to secure a place in heaven, in Buddhist thinking?' I asked.

'We are told that there are eighteen levels of hell,' said Christy, 'and that life is a cycle – humans are always reincarnating and coming back as something else. But if we do good things on earth, the higher chance we will have of reaching heaven, or at least of not being in such a bad level of hell. In Chinese culture, of course, it's the worst kind of curse to reach the eighteenth level of hell – nobody wants to reincarnate as a cockroach – everyone wants to come back at least as a human.'

Christy paused, and I smiled with her, trying briefly to imagine life as a cockroach. 'When you prayed at the temple, who did you pray to?' I asked.

'There are different types of deity,' explained Christy. 'And they rule different parts of life and the home, so we prayed to the one we needed. The kitchen god takes care of the kitchen. The reproduction god helps with reproduction. Then there's a god who helps you to fight, and a god who helps you to make wealth. In August, especially, there is a "hungry ghost" festival. People burn incense in public places, and leave out small bits of food, to appease the ghosts. I remember feeling very fearful during August, every year, when I was a child. In that month, they say that the ghosts are released from hell and they are up to no good, here on the earth. My mother used to tell me to be careful of ashes from the fire. Don't let them float in front of you, she said, and don't step on the ashes, or the ghosts could hurt you. There are always more deaths and funerals in August. I was very scared during elementary school. I would watch TV programmes about all the deities and gods. Then, as a teenager, I started watching horror movies and tapes of black magic in Thailand. I knew there were ghosts. I had a very acute sense of the spirit world. And there were so many gods to pray to . . . but we didn't believe that there was one god overall, who rules everything.'

Christy then told us about her mother, who was a very devout woman. 'My mother was always praying to a god,' she said. 'She was not just asking for things, but also giving thanks. She was very loyal and faithful to the deity. Perhaps I'm a little bit like her. As a child, I remember that I developed a deep attachment to the deity. At one point, my grandmother became very ill, so I knelt before the deity every day and I cried out for healing for my grandmother. I was emotionally attached to the deity. I was very faithful. Every day I would burn joss sticks and incense to the deity, morning and evening, like my mother, for years. But one day I wondered why we had to offer the deity food, and I asked my mother, "Why do we do this?" It was just an innocent question, I wanted to know. My mother said I mustn't ask so many questions – I would offend the gods.'

'Did you have other questions about life and the gods, as you were growing up?' I asked.

'Mostly I wanted to know about my purpose,' said Christy, ordering another dish from the waiter. 'What am I doing here?' she said. 'Where did I come from? Where am I headed?' Christy explained to us that she kept asking the questions – especially the one about where she came from. In all those years she could never find an answer. She remembers learning about evolution in science at high school. That made her happy for about two weeks. But then she started to question again and felt dissatisfied. Where did the first amoeba come from? Or where did the first particle come from? It seemed so random. 'The more I studied biology,' she said, 'the more I thought that there must be a designer.'

'So there you were, praying to the family deity,' I said, 'and wondering where you came from, or why you were here. What was it that brought about change?'

'Everything changed when I was about 15,' said Christy. 'I had a close friend who had a really bad temper. He used to torture cats with a group of the boys. He would tell ghost stories on youth camps. He couldn't control himself. Then one day he became a Christian. I was shocked. He came from a Buddhist-Taoist background like me. I noticed that he changed dramatically after he became a Christian. His temper disappeared. So, of course, I wanted to know how. What power was it that could change someone like that? I'd never seen it before. After he became a Christian, he would begin to swear like before, and then he would stop himself. I'd never thought it was possible to change like that. So I wanted to know who, or what, could bring change like that.'

'What did he say?' I asked.

'He told me about Jesus,' said Christy. 'He started by telling me that there was a Creator God, a designer. He told me the story about Adam and Eve. I thought it was a beautiful story, but maybe it was like a fairy tale. I wasn't sure. And at the same time as he was telling me, I noticed some other people doing Christian street evangelism. They were quite intrusive and I hated that, so I avoided them. I didn't really understand it.

'But then in my late teens,' said Christy, 'I would sometimes stay overnight at the beach with my friends. One night, I was lying on the sand, staring at the stars in the sky, and I asked my female friend, "Where did the stars come from? And where did I come from?" My friend said, "God made you." So I said, "Where did God come from?" She said, "God is God." To me, it sounded like a simple answer. It was Christmas Eve, 1991. I pondered it for three days. Then on the third day, I was at the airport with my friend again. We were often at the airport, it was one of our favourite haunts. I said to my friend, "I would like to know this God who made me."

'My friend led me in the "sinner's prayer",' said Christy, 'but I didn't understand the prayer, mainly because I didn't think I was a sinner. I thought I was a good girl. I was aspiring to be a social worker. I helped people. So I didn't understand it, but I prayed the prayer with her, and I received Jesus. But mostly I was thinking about the other things she said. If God made me, he must have made me for a purpose. He must have made me for a reason and meaning. What was my purpose and meaning? After we prayed, my friend gave me a Bible. I didn't have one before and I devoured it. It was the New King James Version, in English, so it was not an easy read. But I read it . . . and it was full of life! I had never read such teaching before. I started with the Gospels. I loved it. I couldn't understand everything, but there was life. I couldn't stop reading it. I was intrigued. Jesus was not like anyone I had ever met. But I still didn't understand sin, or my need for a saviour.

'Every day before that,' explained Christy, 'I used to pray to the deity. I used to burn the joss sticks, morning and night. But then after I started reading the Bible I wondered if I should continue burning the joss sticks if there was a Creator God. No one had told me before that there was just one God . . . and I was fearful of offending the deity if I stopped and worshipped another God.'

'So what did you do?' I asked.

'I asked my friend . . . if I worship just one God and I pray to him and I believe in him, will he protect me from the deity? I can't remember what my friend said but, at the same time, I had a feeling that I didn't want to burn the joss sticks anymore. My desire went. Then I told my mum that I didn't want to do it anymore and she was very upset. She said the deity would be offended. But then she told me to wait to make my mind up. She said that I would one day get married (to a Buddhist-Taoist man, presumably) and I must follow my husband's religion.'

Christy and I looked at each other at this point in the story. We smiled, knowing that mothers, however well-meaning and lovely, don't always know the long-term plan in regards to future husbands.

'But all of that time,' said Christy, 'I was attracted to the Creator God, so I started to do tricks. I kept burning the joss sticks to the deity but, as I burned the sticks, I would sing Christian songs out loud. It was my way of trying to get out of the situation. My mum said that I would offend the gods and get myself in trouble. But I said I was attracted to the Creator God. Then she said that I could stop burning joss sticks if I wanted to, but I mustn't go to the Christian church. She forbade me from going. I really wanted to go to church, but I couldn't go against her wishes so, instead, I went to the Saturday night fellowship. I told my mother every Saturday night that I was meeting my friends, and I went secretly to the fellowship for two years.'

'Was there a point during that time where the Christian message made more sense to you?' I asked.

'Yes,' said Christy. 'During those two years, I signed up for a camp. It was a Sunday school teacher's training camp. I was not a Sunday school teacher but I went anyway. I remember a speaker asking the question, "Where is Jesus now?" I said that Jesus was in heaven. He said yes, and Jesus was in my heart. That same day, in the evening, another speaker asked the same question, "Where is Jesus now?" And that's when I realised I needed to pray again. I understood, then, what I had not understood two years earlier. So I prayed again. I said, "Lord, you have my heart. I'm sorry. I'm going to follow you." After that, it was a gradual process to understand that I was a sinner and there was no other way to God than to trust in Jesus.'

'Did you still occasionally think you were a good girl?' I asked, mostly interested because, at the same age, I had also thought I was a good girl.

'I did a bit,' said Christy, 'but then I slowly realised that there were times when I lied, or didn't have the best of intentions, or when I was self-delusional. I realised that before, I would tell myself that I was good and kind, yet underneath I actually wasn't. So it was a slow conviction of the Holy Spirit, over time. Then I began to realise that I truly needed Jesus as my saviour. I couldn't do it myself. I couldn't be good enough.'

After two years of secretly going to the Saturday night fellowship, Christy said that she began to want to go public with her family about her faith. So she asked her friends at church to pray for her – that she would be allowed to go to church on Sundays openly.

'Then one day on a Sunday,' said Christy, 'I was lying on my bed and praying, and I felt God say to me, "What are you doing lying on your bed? You are asking your friends to pray for you, and you are not ready to go to church. You should be ready to go to church." So that's when I got up, and I dressed and I went downstairs and I asked my mother, "Mum, can I please go to church?" My mother said, "No, you cannot. I will throw you out of the house if you go to church." So then I went back up to my room and I read the Scriptures and I sang and I worshipped God by myself, in my room.'

A week went by and the same thing happened. It was Sunday, and Christy felt that she should be ready to go to church, even if she couldn't go, so she got up and dressed and went downstairs and asked her mother if she could go to church. Her mother said no again, so Christy went back upstairs and read the Scriptures and sang in her room, by herself. The same thing happened Sunday after Sunday. Many weeks went by. Then it was Easter Sunday. Christy said she *really* wanted to go to church. So she went downstairs and asked her mother again. She begged to be allowed to go to church. She said, "Mum, it's Easter Sunday! It's a special day. Please can I go to church?" And her mother said no, she couldn't.

'I was so angry,' admitted Christy. 'I stormed out of the house and down the front steps. My mother came after me. She said, "If you go to church, you will not be allowed to come back to this house." I kept walking for a while and then I felt the Lord telling me to turn back, so I said to the Lord, "Why? I want to go to church in a building." But at the same time, I couldn't refuse the voice, so I went back home and I said sorry to my mother for raising my voice. Then I went quietly to my room. The next Sunday, I got dressed again, and I went downstairs and I said to my mother, "Mum, I would like to go to church." And my mother said yes, I could go.'

I paused and stared at Christy. 'Wow! What do you think caused the change?'

Christy smiled. 'It was the happiest day of my life. I went to church. All the people who were praying for me were so happy. I was in church, with my parent's blessing. Later I found out that it was my grandmother, who isn't even a believer, who talked to my mother and suggested that my mother allow me to go to church. I also realised that it was the right prompt on Easter Sunday – to go back home and to say sorry to my mother. I think that was part of it.'

'After that, how did you grow in your understanding of your faith?' I asked.

'I cherished every meeting I could go to,' said Christy. 'My fondest memories were the group of young people that I met with. We were praying together, singing our lungs out praising God, sharing our lives together, and learning the Word of God together. I grew primarily through the discipleship of a mentor who mentored a group of us. He had been a drug addict and a gangster, and he had been imprisoned for his crimes, but the Lord turned him around while he was in prison. He loved the Lord passionately, and he was very firm with us in terms of spiritual disciplines and particularly about reaching out to others who did not yet know Christ. He would go door-to-door to share the gospel, and he role-modelled for us a selfless giving of ourselves to the Lord's service. As well as that, I started to pray more. Over time, I started to see that prayer is a conversation. I can pray and ask. And God will change and influence me, every day.'

During all that time, Christy explained that she really wanted to be baptised, but her mother said she had to wait until she was 21. So Christy waited. 'On the day of my baptism, I felt like a bride,' she said. 'I beamed with joy at finally being able to publicly identify with the Lord in his death and resurrection.' It was a wonderful day, she said, and her sister was also able to be there.

By then, Christy had graduated as a social worker, and she spent the next few years working in a family service centre in Singapore, serving a variety of young people in need, as well as couples struggling with their marriages and parenting, and those suffering from domestic violence and mental illness. In 1999 when Christy was 24, she met her husband, Nan, and they married three years later in 2002. Nan was also a Christian, but to Christy's mother it was actually a relief. Christy's mother liked him and she trusted him. Christy and Nan lived with his parents for a while and then they moved into their own flat, in north-east Singapore.

'And then five years later, you moved to the Middle East?' I asked.

'Yes,' said Christy. 'I went on a short-term mission trip to Chiang Rai [Thailand] when I was 19, and I was deeply moved by it. I told myself that I could do this for the rest of my life. Then I carried that desire with me for a long time, not knowing if I would serve overseas alone, or as a married woman. Then four years after we were married, the Lord confirmed his call to both of us, to serve him cross-culturally overseas.

'So we applied to go with a Christian organisation, and they found us an opportunity to work in the Middle East. Amazingly, my mother didn't object. She thought it was OK, because my husband wanted to go. Actually, it was God's leading and a joint decision by both of us. But my mother didn't object . . . we sold our flat in Singapore so that we could go debt-free. We ended up serving in the Middle East for six years, from 2007 to 2013.'

At that point in the story, I pictured Christy and Nan flying in to their Middle Eastern city from the shining streets of Singapore. They must have seemed, initially at least, a really long way from home, and from the local restaurants with such a lovely variety of *Zi Char*. As I asked her more about those years, Christy began to bubble over. I could tell that she had at least a hundred stories from her time in that city. 'What was the best thing about those years?' I asked.

'It was being able to experience God in deep ways,' she said. 'I was serving in an African refugee school, doing social work and counselling and building up a local team to provide psychosocial support to their own community, and building friendships with local women. Nan acted as the principal of a high school and he taught the

Bible to adult refugees. The best thing, though, was the relationships we built over the years – with the local Christians and Muslims. We saw the Christian faith lived out in broader ways than in Singapore. In Singapore, our brand of Christianity can seem quite narrow, or quite influenced by the West. But in that city, we saw the ancient church. Within the ancient church there were many who had a living relationship with Jesus. Then there was the international church and the African church,' Christy smiled, remembering. 'It was all so colourful.'

'Did you have struggles during those years?' I asked.

'Yes,' said Christy. 'We were in the city from 2007 to 2013, and the Arab Spring began in 2011. It spread across the country. There were millions of people on the streets, protesting. As Singaporeans, we had never had riots. We were so sheltered. In that city, we heard gunshots from our flat. Some people were released from prison to create unrest. There were tanks in the street and people frantically buying goods. The automatic teller machines ran out of money. And God spoke to us. He said, "You shall not leave in haste."[1] The refugees were our friends. They knew that the Singaporean government could help us, but it wouldn't help them. The refugees had nobody to help them. So we stayed, and it deepened our relationships with all of them – the Muslims and the Christians. It was so good to be on that soil during that time – it added so much richness. The active fighting lasted a month but the struggle for freedom and justice lingered for a long time. The topple was bloody – many people died. The local church was desperate, we were all on our knees, praying. Millions of people had their lives at stake. Anything could have happened.'

I nodded, trying to imagine the crowds on the streets and the uncertainty. 'Looking back,' I said, 'what did you learn during those years?'

'Mostly about gratitude,' said Christy. 'At the same time as the revolution, there were government elections going on back in Singapore. I remember one night we were Skyping a family member, and she was talking about the election issues in Singapore. People were complaining against the government because the trains were sometimes late. But there we were, with a revolution and enormous injustice and corruption and instability all around us. I could not help but feel we have so much to learn about gratitude, as well as our responsibility as Singaporeans, blessed with so much.'

Christy said that she and Nan moved back to Singapore in June 2013. It was at that point that she took up a new role with the same mission organisation that helped send them out, helping other people to find ways to serve God in the neediest parts of the world, where the workers are the fewest.

'What do you think the challenge is for Singaporean Christians today?' I asked.

'Singaporean Christians,' said Christy, 'can seem quite motivated by safety. If I tell them about the needs in the Middle East or in Central Asia, for example, they will say, "Is it safe?" They want to know if it's safe to go; and it makes me think that there is a security gospel being unwittingly preached in Singapore, as well as a prosperity gospel. Although many believers here love the Lord and are actively serving him, they can seem to think that their primary concern is to stay safe. Or that God will keep us safe. Where in the Bible does Jesus promise safety? What does he really say? What if Singaporean Christians realised our role in serving the nations, beyond what we are already engaged in? From Singapore, we can travel easily, and we have good political standing with most countries . . . so we could give up more, we could serve more, we could mobilise the church more, in order to bring God's love to the people of every nation.'

I agreed with Christy, and wondered whether the security gospel was also being preached quietly in Australia. By then, though, we had nearly finished our *Zi Char*, so I looked at the notes I had made. 'And what do you think now about your purpose and meaning in life?' I asked.

'I don't think God has given me a blueprint for my life,' said Christy, 'although he certainly speaks often enough for me to take a step of faith at a time. But it hasn't always been clear. I haven't always felt God saying, "This is what you must do." It's more about understanding who God is, and that he made me. He is the great designer. He pre-existed everything. And I know where I'm heading. I know that there is eternal life with him, and I know that I'm going there. In between all of that, I don't need to know everything. I have a loving Father who will lead me and speak to me through the Scriptures and the people around me. He won't abandon me. It's an adventure. Some people think Christianity is boring. To me it's freedom from the power of sin. I have freedom to choose what is right and good, just like my friend who had the anger problem. He chooses not to sin. It's like that every day, for all of us. We choose and he helps us. I don't know what's ahead of me but I know God will lead me . . . and he will give me the freedom to obey him.'

I agreed with her. 'What about your parents, now?' I said. 'How are they?'

'They're both well,' said Christy. 'They're not Christians yet, but I always use the word "yet" when I describe them. I often see people as being "pre-believers", and that includes my parents. I know that my beloved, devoted mother will show the same, if not more devotion, to our worthy Lord, when she comes to faith in him. Then her life will attract many more people to Jesus.'

By then, we had finished our meal, so we began to organise the bill. We walked back to our hotel on Bencoolen Street, Singapore, and said 'goodbye' and 'thank you' to Christy. As we did so, she gave us a parting gift – a jar of Singaporean *kaya* spread, made of coconut cream and pandan leaves, to take home with us and to have on our toast in Australia. It smelled wonderful. Later, as I packed it into our bags, I prayed that it would remind me of Christy's story, and the encouragement she received . . . and the truth for all of us, that sometimes the most surprising witness to Jesus can be the genuine and lasting change we observe in our closest friends. May we all continue to be, and have, those kinds of friends.

5

It all came flooding back to me

Richard – Central Australia

Richard Driver Jakamarra was born in Phillip Creek in May 1950. Back then, Phillip Creek was a tiny aboriginal mission, 50 kilometres north of Tennant Creek, right in the centre of the Northern Territory, Australia – dry and flat and dusty, or that's how it appears to someone like me. For Richard, of course, and for his people, who have connected with this land for thousands of years, it's home. Richard himself has lived in the Northern Territory all of his life. He's a part of the Warlpiri tribal people, and he's been one of the leaders at the indigenous church in Tennant Creek for thirty-three years. He's also been blind for thirty-one years.

I was keen to meet Richard and to hear more of his faith story, so a friend and I travelled to Tennant Creek in the last week of September. We chose September because we thought it wouldn't be too hot, and we could possibly cope with the heat, as well as the harshness of the outback. Of course, it turned out to be the hottest September on record. We picked up a hire car in Alice Springs and we drove directly north for 508 kilometres, through a flat, straight, burned red landscape. I stared at the heat haze in front of us. Occasionally, the wind picked up and the red dust swirled all around our car. The temperature reached 40 degrees and we turned the air conditioning to high. There were occasional shrubs and shady trees. It went on and on – the straight long road, the red dust around us, and the balls of spinifex grass, blowing across the road. By 6 p.m., though, the sun was low on the horizon and we were passing Karlu Karlu on our left – the area around the Devils Marbles.

We stopped the car and got out to take photos of the huge marble-like rocks. It was quiet and beautiful, and there was space everywhere. The light on the red rocks was breathtaking. We smiled for the photos, and I breathed in deeply for the first time in ages. 'Perhaps we will find something surprising here,' I thought. We got back in the car, and kept driving straight, and arrived in Tennant Creek in the dark. It was a small town of about three thousand people. None of the shops seemed to be open. We found our way to our cabin at the Outback Caravan Park, turned the fan on to high, and fell fast asleep.

The next morning, we woke to another heat-hazy day. A mutual friend, who worked with the Australian Indigenous Ministries (AIM), had organised to introduce us to Richard, at the AIM church building, on the corner of Standley Street and the Stuart Highway. We followed his instructions and we arrived at a small building made of tin, surrounded by red dirt and rocks, and heat haze. Our friend from AIM and Richard Driver also arrived at the same time. They got out of the car, and our friend led Richard, who was using his stick, towards the building. We shook hands, introducing ourselves, and went inside. It was slightly cooler indoors.

'Richard always sits here,' said our friend, pointing to the front pew. 'He's been sitting here on this same pew every week for thirty-three years.' Richard sat down on his front pew and I pulled over a plastic chair, and asked him about his childhood.

'I grew up in Phillip Creek Mission,' said Richard, staring ahead of him, his eyes closed, but clearly seeing something in his imagination. 'It was an aboriginal settlement run by the government. AIM was there too. I used to milk the goats and eat bush tucker,' he smiled. 'We all did, the yams that grew along the creek – big yams. My father, he drove the truck. His country was out west – Jipiranpa, out Willowra way. But then my family came to this area around Tennant Creek because of the Coniston massacre.[1] My father met my mother, I think, at Phillip Creek. She also came from out Willowra way.

'In Phillip Creek I went to preschool and grade 1 . . . And we lived in a mud house. There were six mud houses as well as humpies. But there wasn't much rain. The people used to cart water to Phillip Creek from the windmill at the telegraph station. That was the first white fella infrastructure out here. But it was expensive carting water, so one day the government put us all in a big truck and they moved us to Warrabri. My old man drove the truck. We moved to a settlement at Warrabri – that place is called Alekarenge now – it's the Kaytete name.'

We all nodded. I had read up on Alekarenge before the trip, and we had even driven past the turnoff the day before. Richard explained to us that he went to school out there, and he liked reading and writing. 'They taught us to play Australian Rules Football out there,' he said. 'I was "ruckman". After we played, we would go hunting, with my brothers and sisters. We followed the old people around. They showed us how to hunt for kangaroos, and how to find bush tucker – berries to eat. Sometimes we caught zebra finches. We ate them up. And rock melons from the garden. Then they showed us how to track the goanna. Sometimes we ate the goanna – cooked it on the fire, ate it whole.'

We all smiled. Goanna – a monitor lizard – is a delicacy. Richard explained that he left school in 1964, when he was 14 years old. 'There weren't any high schools or colleges then,' he said, 'so I did odd jobs. Sometimes I got droving work on big cattle stations out east. I used to ride the horses and move the stock, with my mates. We'd sleep on swags and eat rations. Then sometimes we got work up in Darwin, for the army. But also in that time that's when I first heard about the Lord Jesus. I went to Sunday school when I was at Alekarenge, and then I went to a Christian group when I was a teenager. I heard about the Word of God.'

'Do you remember what you thought about Jesus, back then?' I asked.

'Yes,' said Richard. 'I heard about Jesus through a Baptist minister. He used to come to our school and he taught us the Bible. From an early age I heard about the Lord Jesus. I went to church a lot when we were in Alekarenge. I used to lead the singing sometimes. It was good.'

But back then, in the 1960s, the indigenous people of Australia were not formally recognised as citizens. They were restricted in where they could live and work. In Tennant Creek, for example, indigenous people were not allowed to enter the town at certain times of the day, or live there permanently. Children, particularly those of mixed race, were often taken away from their families and placed in government care. Aboriginal land was not recognised. But it all changed in 1967. A referendum was called by the Holt government and Australians voted overwhelmingly to change the constitution relating to indigenous Australians. Most importantly, aboriginal people could now become citizens of Australia, and in turn, that meant that they could go wherever they wanted to go, be paid equal wages, and also, drink alcohol.

'I don't know what we were before that,' said Richard, 'but in 1967, we became citizens of Australia. That's when I started to drink alcohol. I was 17. I turned away from the Lord because grog was available. Before that I used to go to church a lot, I used to do the singing, but after I started drinking I only went sporadically. I became an alcoholic. I knew that I was doing wrong things . . . but I couldn't stop. I tried to give up the drink three times, in my own strength, but I couldn't do it. I failed. I was a slave to alcohol. I had jobs, many jobs – droving and in the army – but I couldn't keep them. I kept losing the jobs. It was a big problem.'

In 1980, when Richard was 29, he explained that he was still living in Alekarenge, and that's when he found Phyllis Napangardi. Phyllis was from the north, and from the right skin group, which is very important in aboriginal culture. Apparently, this complex and ancient system – eight female and eight male groups, in each tribal group – is understood by everyone, from when they're very young: which skin group they belong to, and which skin group everyone else belongs to, and to whom they are connected, and to whom they can be married, or not. The skin groups are partly determined by the names of each parent; however, the child is always in a different skin group to their parent. For thousands of years, the system has conveyed information about how the generations are allowed to interact with each other, and it has protected them genetically, which in turn has contributed to their claim to be the longest continuing culture on this earth. 'I'm a Jakamarra,' said Richard, 'and Phyllis is Napangardi, so we're from the right skin group. We can marry, and we found each other in Tennant Creek around 1980.

'But the whole social system, it's complicated,' said Richard, slowly. 'It's about kinship. At Alekarenge, different nations were mixed together. Some of them had fled from Phillip Creek after the Coniston massacre. Now in Tennant Creek there are many different people groups – the Warlpiri, the Warumungu, the Alyawarr, and the Kaytete are the main ones, with many other tribes from the outlying areas . . . and you have to marry the right skin group – not your own skin group, the right skin group. We know what skin we are and there's always a connection through your skin group. So I married Phyllis Napangardi and she already had two children and we adopted one child, and then we had one child of our own, Michael. But it was before that, that God started to work in my life.'

In 1984, Richard explained that he and Phyllis were living in Tennant Creek. Work was sporadic and they were both drinking heavily. 'Then one night I had a drinking session,' said Richard, 'and I was drunk. I was sleeping in my home. I don't remember much, but someone came in through the window. That person was one of our people. And he cut me with a knife around my neck.' Richard paused in the story and he marked a line all around the right side of his neck, showing where the knife went. 'When I came to, I was lying in the Alice Springs Hospital. They had taken me there in the Royal Flying Doctor aircraft. Phyllis said there was blood everywhere.

'I was lying in the Intensive Care Unit of Alice Springs Hospital and the doctor came to my bed and he said to me, "Richard, you're very, very lucky to be alive. If the knife had gone in another half an inch, you wouldn't be here." This sort of scared me, it frightened me. While I was lying there, all those things that I'd heard in Sunday school came flooding back to me. I knew about the Lord, and I knew that if I'd died, I'd have ended up in hell, because I was that far away from the Lord, and this thought got me thinking while I was in the hospital.

'A few days later, they moved me from Intensive Care to ward nine, and it was there in ward nine that the Lord began to touch my life; he began to speak to me, not in a way I could understand, but he touched my heart, and my life, and I knew that the Lord was doing this to me. It was there that a hospital chaplain came to see me. He wanted to know if any of us patients wanted to have a prayer time or a Bible study with him. I volunteered. I went with the chaplain, and one other patient went as well, and the chaplain prayed for us. I didn't give my life to the Lord yet. But it started. I started to think that if I survived, I would serve the Lord for the rest of my life.'

Meanwhile, back in Tennant Creek, Phyllis had also been stabbed by the intruder, and so had two of their friends who were staying with them at the time. One of the friends had somehow managed to call the ambulance to get help for all four. 'He was one of our people,' repeated Richard. 'That man, I went to school with him. He was a mate, but he'd also been drinking. That's what happens with grog.'

After a week, Richard was discharged from Alice Springs Hospital and he was flown back to Tennant Creek. 'I knew I wanted to give my life to the Lord,' said Richard, 'and when I got back to Tennant Creek, it was the same week that the AIM were opening this building here. It was 1984 – thirty-three years ago.'

Richard indicated the place where we sat, with the tin walls, and the few pictures hung there. 'The same building,' he said. 'They invited me to the opening of this, and I went. It was held outside – we sat outside, over there. I sat up the back on the left, near my friend Cedric Tennyson. Cedric had been a fighter, and an alcoholic as well, but he'd given his life to the Lord two years earlier. He sat next to me.

'Then at the end of the service, the speaker – he was an aboriginal church leader – he asked if anyone would like to give their hearts to the Lord. I turned to Cedric and I asked him if I should . . . But Cedric told me that that was between me and the Lord. He said he couldn't decide for me. Then I got up and I went forward. I asked the speaker to pray for me and I accepted the Lord Jesus as my personal saviour.

'It changed me,' said Richard. 'I went forward thirty-three years ago, in this same place where we're sitting now.' Richard smiled, 'Except it was outdoors.' He pointed again at the red dirt outside. 'It was September but it wasn't as hot as it is now. There were a few of us who gave our lives to the Lord Jesus that day, including me and my friend Michael Jones Jampin. He and I grew up together in Alekarenge. From that time, I haven't looked back.'

'Did things change immediately?' I asked.

'Yes,' said Richard. 'I came back from Alice Springs and I knew I didn't want to drink alcohol anymore. There was money at the post office, I knew that, I could have bought the grog, but I had no urge to do it. The urge was gone. Before, I was a drunkard. I couldn't keep a job down, and I'd tried to give up the grog before . . . Then the Lord helped me to give up all those rubbish things that I couldn't do in my own strength – like alcoholism, for instance, and cigarette smoking. I gave it all up. In my strength I couldn't do it, but I found freedom in the Lord Jesus. He set me free.

'Then a few days later, I took Phyllis to see Cedric Tennyson, who was one of the church leaders. I wanted her to see him. Cedric knew how to talk to people about the Lord. I didn't. I was a new Christian then, so I didn't know how to do it. But he talked to her. He counselled her to give up the grog. And Phyllis gave up drinking right then, and she gave her life to the Lord too . . .

'Then in 1988, on 7 August, we dedicated our marriage to the Lord. It was in this building we did it, in front of all the people.' Richard smiled again, remembering the occasion. 'She was illiterate, Phyllis. But there was no one I'd rather be in the bush with. She knew everything about the bush. And we dedicated our marriage to the Lord right here.'

'What about work?' I asked. 'Did that change as well?'

'I found work,' said Richard. 'In the past, I had government jobs offered to me, but I could never keep those jobs down, because of my foolishness. After I was saved, my life changed. I was offered a job with the local aboriginal council in Tennant Creek – the Julalikari Council. I drove trucks for them and I kept the job. It helped me a lot. I could support my family without relying on benefits. We began to attend church, and it was good.'

I nodded. 'But something changed after that?'

'Yes,' said Richard. 'In 1986, I went blind. I didn't know what it was at first. It started slowly. I couldn't see very well. Then I couldn't see anything. I went to see a doctor in Tennant Creek who said there was nothing they could do. Then another one of the church leaders here suggested that I go and see a doctor in Sydney that had fixed his eyes. That man in Sydney was Professor Fred Hollows. My friend from AIM, Richard Davies, brought me to Sydney and I saw Professor Fred Hollows at the Prince of Wales Hospital in Randwick. I had a scan and they found something inside my head that was destroying me. It was a brain tumour, pressing on the optic nerve. I can still remember what Professor Fred Hollows said. He said to me: "We've got to do something about this, Richard, we've got to get this brain tumour out of your head, otherwise it will kill you in six months and you'll go mad with the pain." So they took me to Prince Henry Hospital in La Perouse. That's where they did the operation.'

While Richard was waiting for the operation, his friend from AIM came to visit him on the ward. As the friend approached Richard's hospital bed, another patient called the friend over. The patient asked the AIM friend if he knew the 'blackfella' over there. The AIM friend said that he did. The other patient said, 'He's the most amazing man I've ever met! All week, we've been in here and the blackfella has been feeling his way around the ward, talking to all the patients, one by one. When he came to me, we had a yarn for about an hour, and then he asked me if he could pray for me. I've got a back problem, and he's got a brain tumour that could kill him, and he wants to pray for me! What's going on?'

The other patient looked perplexed and the AIM friend nodded again and said, 'Yes, my friend is amazing! He's a Christian. That's why he cares for you and that's why he wants to pray for you. It's because he's let Jesus into his life.'

The other patient was still baffled. 'You don't understand,' he said. 'I'm the police sergeant at Redfern. It's the toughest part of Sydney . . . and I never thought I'd praise a blackfella! I've been calling the station all day and telling the other constables to come and meet him. It's amazing!'

Then Richard had his operation. Prior to being wheeled in, the doctors explained to him that they would try to remove the tumour, but they would not be able to bring his sight back. They also said that Richard could possibly die in the operation. Richard was not fussed. 'As I went into the operation room, I had that peace,' he said, 'because I knew the Lord was with me. I wasn't afraid of dying or anything like that. One of the other patients said to me, "I don't think you'll make it." And I thought to myself, "That's what you think. Let's wait and see what the Lord will do . . ."

'I wasn't scared of what was going to happen. There was a peace all over me – the peace of the Lord. It says that in John 14, verse 27. It says, 'My peace I give you . . . Do not let your hearts be troubled". I had that peace, and when I came to, I said to myself, "I am alive." I knew that the Lord had helped me, and he had helped the surgeons that did the operation on me.'

By then, it was the middle of 1986 and Richard was 36 years old. He spent another four months in Prince of Wales Hospital in Sydney having radiotherapy. Before the operation and during that time, Phyllis was able to visit him in the hospital, with their baby, Michael. Then in January 1987, Richard returned home to Tennant Creek, and to Phyllis and his family. 'It was good to be back home,' he said, 'but I thought, that's it. I'm blind. I'm no use to anyone. I can't preach anymore. I'm no use to the Lord.'

Unbeknown to Richard, though, it wasn't over. The same AIM friend who had visited him in hospital had had an idea. He'd brought Richard a set of cassette tapes, with the Good News Bible recorded on them using an Australian voice, produced by the Bible Society.

'I started with Romans,' said Richard. 'I decided to memorise verses. And I did. I found I could do it, in the hospital. My friend helped me. Then when I got back to Tennant Creek, I kept going.

On Wednesdays at church, we'd have sharing nights, and one Wednesday, I went forward and shared verses from the Scriptures. It helped people. Then I began to memorise long passages, and then sermons. I began to work for the Lord that way – preaching and even sharing Bible verses for my people and explaining what they meant and helping our people at funeral services too. Prior to losing my sight, I used to help with the preaching, and I'd put notes on paper, so I thought I would never be able to preach again. But the Lord proved me wrong. He gave me an amazing gift. It began with the cassette player, but that became obsolete. Then we had CDs. Then another machine came onto the market. It's a MegaVoice. It's helped me a lot. Here, have a look at it.' Richard pulled a small machine out of his pocket and passed it to us. 'It was given to me so that I could help my own people in Tennant Creek.'

We looked at the MegaVoice. It was a tiny machine, smaller than my phone, and solar-powered. As Richard pressed each button, the Scriptures began, in an Australian voice. A need had been recognised to produce the Bible in audio form for people living in places without electricity, particularly in Asia and Africa . . . but it was also perfect for Richard, in Tennant Creek, Central Australia. It was the same spoken version that he was used to hearing on cassette, with the same Australian accent!

'What part of the Bible are you listening to at the moment?' I asked.

'Psalm 121,' said Richard, straight away. He put down the MegaVoice and began to tell us the psalm, slowly and carefully, with his eyes still closed.

I look to the mountains;
    where will my help come from?
My help will come from the LORD,
    who made heaven and earth.
He will not let you fall;
    your protector is always awake.
The protector of Israel
    never dozes or sleeps.

The LORD will guard you;
    he is by your side to protect you.
The sun will not hurt you during the day,
    nor the moon during the night.
The LORD will protect you from all danger;
    he will keep you safe.
He will protect you as you come and go
    now and forever.

(GNB)

As Richard spoke, he didn't stumble over any of the words. He spoke clearly and beautifully, each word perfectly pronounced. It was almost as if he was reading the passage out loud with a perfectly bound Bible in his hands, in front of him. I said that to him. Could he somehow see the words in his head, as he read?

'No,' he answered me. 'I just remember it. That's how I do it.'

For the last thirty years, Richard has been memorising the Bible and helping to lead the small indigenous congregation at Tennant Creek with the other leaders. In the late 1980s, he attended short Bible courses, and then in 1995 he was the main speaker at the Katherine Christian Convention. In 2001, he was recognised as the Tennant Creek 'Citizen of the Year', for his service to the church and to local aboriginals through the indigenous church. Now, Richard is 67 and still preaches regularly.

'Sometimes fifty people come on a Sunday,' he said. 'It's the biggest church in Tennant Creek. And I'm not the only leader. There are several other fellas – including my friends Michael Jones Jampin and Cedric Tennyson and David Duggie and Geoffrey Shannon and Jimmy Brodie. We work together and we take turns leading and preaching so that the Word of God is given to our people.

'Our people don't just come here from Tennant Creek, they come from all the surrounding outstations, the cattle stations and the other communities. They come in and they join with us and have fellowship with us, because we serve the same God. But a lot of our people are still transit people, they move from place to place; sometimes they go out hunting or to visit relatives in the Barkly area, so our numbers change. Sometimes we preach in our own language, or other languages we know. There are about thirteen aboriginal languages in Tennant Creek. The main one is Warumungu . . . They're all very different. I don't understand all the others, they're very hard. A lot of our people are still illiterate. Even at sharing nights, we get some people come forward who can't read, but they share in their Christian songs in their own languages. Or they put Bible teaching on canvas, on artwork.'

At this point, we looked at the artwork hung on the walls. Then Richard explained to us that on Tuesday nights they have men's and women's groups at the church at 6 p.m. as well as sharing nights on Wednesdays. It happened to be a Tuesday, so Richard asked if we would like to come back that evening to the groups. We both said, 'Yes, we'd love to come.' By that time in our conversation, the temperature was back up to 40 degrees, and Richard was looking like he needed a break, so we took our cue to leave. We shook hands with him, and thanked him very much, as he was led back out the door by his friend.

It was midday, and my friend and I had six hours to fill in Tennant Creek, in a September heatwave, with a hot, dry wind. So, first of all, we drove to the outskirts of the town to get an idea of where we were. We took photos of the straight dirt roads and the red dust all around us. Then we found a hill and we left our air-conditioned car to climb to the top of the hill and take more photos, and watch the black kites circle around the rubbish heaps. By then, of course, we were fairly hot, so we got back in the car and went to the cultural centre on the main street of Tennant Creek. The centre is called Nyinkka Nyunyu, and it was set up, in part, by Richard's friend Michael Jones Jampin.

It was cool inside the cultural centre. We picked up an audio tour guide and began to walk around the displays, reading the stories quietly. It was sobering. The pictures and dioramas, all from the perspective of the local indigenous people, told many stories – of their vast, harsh land, their dreaming, their nomadic way of life, their bush tucker, their connection to the land . . . and then the gradual appearance of the

Europeans, the destruction of soil and waterholes by cattle and camels, the misunderstanding, the people displaced and ignored, or stolen, and the culture and values that were not well understood or regarded. It was all very complex. There were so many interwoven stories, from the early settlers, the government, the people of the land, the early missionaries, the complex agendas. Now in 2017, it was not over, or easy.

In Tennant Creek, the population of 3,000 people is about two-thirds aboriginal. Many of them live according to cultural norms – they know their skin group and who they can marry, and who they can't. Apparently, even today, if someone is from the wrong skin, they may not look that person in the eye, or say their name out loud, or share any room or space with them. It can cause trouble if there is training in a building. If someone walks in from the wrong skin group, someone else may walk out. There is little paid work in the area, and even less for the young people to do, except for a few jobs on the gas pipeline. There is trouble everywhere, including domestic violence.

My friend and I finished our tour of the cultural centre and went back to our cabin at the Outback Caravan Park. We sat down and had a cool drink and an orange. I felt saddened by the history, and ashamed that I knew so little about the people of the Northern Territory, and their story. I opened my laptop and began to type the first part of Richard's story, as he had described it to us that morning. As I typed, I could hear his voice again. It was soft and humble. Somehow, he didn't tell a tale of bitterness or retribution. He told a story of grace – of what the Lord had done in his life. Even when I had asked him about the day when his people were rounded up by the government and moved from their home in Phillip Creek to Alekarenge, he didn't sound bitter or resentful. It was a part of his story.

That evening, we arrived back at the AIM church building just before 6 p.m. A few people were already gathering. Someone introduced me to Cedric Tennyson and Michael Jones Jampin, and we chatted briefly to them on the stools outside. I especially wanted to know about skins – if someone from the wrong skin comes to church, what happens? Do other people from a different skin group have to leave?

Michael smiled at us. 'We don't let skin rules stop our fellowship in Christ,' he said. 'We follow good traditional ways, like we respect our elders. That's what Christ has done for us. He's made us one family, so there's none of that here. We have unity in Christ, and that means it doesn't matter about our skin, or our family disputes; we're all one in Christ here. We still marry according to our skins, and we follow other cultural rules that are good, but we don't do it if it's contrary to the gospel. We show love to each other, because we know we've been loved.' Michael paused, his face wrinkled in the low-setting sun. 'We still have our problems. But when I first heard the gospel I couldn't believe that God loved me. He loved me! In Romans 5 it says that Jesus died for us while we were sinners. And we're all sinners. We're not perfect. We have troubles. But God loves us. That's what it says in Romans 5.' Michael paused, obviously overcome again by the truth of God's love for him. Then he stretched and got up to greet his long-time friend Richard, who was coming over, using his stick. It was time to meet with the others.

Richard and Michael walked slowly across to the men's group. My friend and I joined the group with the women and children. After the meeting I asked Richard again about his Bible reading. 'Of all the Bible verses that you've read and memorised,' I said, 'is there one that stands out a lot, or that helps you to keep going?'

'Yes,' smiled Richard. 'Proverbs 3:5,6. It says, "Trust in the LORD with all your heart. Never rely on what you think you know. Remember the LORD in everything you do, and he will show you the right way"'(GNB). Richard paused. 'I first heard that Bible verse after I lost my sight. It helped me more than anything. It helped me cope with the blindness. "Lean not on your own understanding", it says. There was one time I remember I was sharing with one of my friends, and I was even thanking the Lord for my blindness. I know it is a very hard thing to do – to thank God for something you don't like, but I knew I had to do it.'

'And is there something that you would like to say to the reader, more than anything?' I asked.

'I want to tell the people what the Lord can do in your life,' said Richard, 'if you give him the chance. Sometimes we feel like we're no more use to anyone . . . Something has happened and it's over. But it's not true, it isn't over, if we let God work in our lives . . . So keep on living for the Lord. Allow him to work in your life, and he will.'

I agreed with Richard, and I realised how profound his words were, given how hard his life had been, and how hard it still was, every day. He had told us earlier that Phyllis had died in 2009 of a heart attack, and that he himself had ongoing bouts of ill-health, on top of his blindness. Yet his parting words to us were about the Lord's work in each of us.

Just as I was about to get back in the car, I asked him one more thing: 'By the way,' I said, 'what happened to the man who stabbed you?'

'He became a Christian a few years later,' smiled Richard. 'He sits next to me in church. We're friends.'

I smiled and thanked him, and we said goodbye. It seemed to me that his story was so humble and true and quiet, lived out in this tiny radius, in the red centre of Australia, among his aboriginal people and his vast land. Within that, no one was waving a big flag, saying, 'Look at Richard!' He had just been looking to the Lord daily, and memorising Bible verses, and encouraging his people, for years.

The next day, my friend and I got back into our hire car and drove back down to Alice Springs – 508 kilometres on that straight red road, with the heat haze all around us. It was quiet. At one point we got out of the car to look at the wild flowers. They were blooming all along the side of the road, red and purple and yellow, thriving in the harsh desert environment. It was spring after all. I thought to myself that it was strange that we hadn't noticed the flowers on the way up. Then when I got back in the car, I saw that red dust was firmly stuck to my skin, and in between my toes. I hoped that it would stay there, and remind me of the story.

6

There would be no more of me

Birgit – Australia

I met Birgit on social media, of all places. She told me that her parents were German and they were atheists. For most of her life, she was quite adamant that she would never have anything to do with the Christian faith, or with Christians, or with the church, at all. She would never go into a church, and she would never get married in one, and she would never have her children christened in one.

That degree of determination interested me immediately, so I arranged to meet Birgit at the Sushi Train restaurant, in Sutherland, south of Sydney, a fortnight later. We introduced ourselves, and then we chose pumpkin sushi, and I asked her more about her story. Birgit said that she was born in Loftus, Sydney, but when she was 2 years old, the family moved back to Germany for five years, to live in the city of Bremen, in the north-west of the country. That meant that when they eventually returned to Tasmania, five years later, Birgit did not fit in. She was seen as the shy kid with the German name, and the German accent and, as well as that, she had buck teeth. Over the next eight years, Birgit's family also moved house five times, and that did not help Birgit's ability to fit in.

'It was hard moving schools,' said Birgit, 'but my dad liked to build. He was a cabinet maker by trade and he built all of our houses, mostly out of brick. My parents would buy a block of land, and then he would build the house, and then they would sell the house, and then they would buy another block of land, and it would start all over again. There was always the next house, or the next block of land, and the next school to enrol in.'

When Birgit was 15, her mother found a hobby farm – five acres of land in Kingston, to the west of the Tasman Bridge. Birgit's mother and father really liked the acreage, so they sold their current house and started building again, this time with the family living in a caravan for five months, while they constructed the new house. The family all stayed on the farm for ten years, along with a goat, a pig, a cow, a bull, chickens, geese, ducks, a vegetable garden and the hay paddock. Birgit's new chores included collecting the eggs and milking the goat.

'Did school become any easier?' I asked.

'I always liked school,' said Birgit, 'but the social aspects were very difficult, especially changing schools at 15. I enjoyed maths and science, and I wanted to go on and study more, especially maths. I liked it because there was a right and a wrong. But after I finished Year 10, my mother said to me that it was time for me to leave school. She said that I would get married in a couple of years, and have children, so what was the point of studying?' Birgit paused. 'So that's when I left school.'

Birgit's mother, Anneliese, had grown up in Germany during the Second World War. Anneliese's father had gone away to the war and never came back. Anneliese herself had left school at 14, and worked as a seamstress before having children in her early twenties, so naturally, Anneliese imagined that Birgit would do the same.

Birgit did not. She left school and found a job at the Wrest Point Casino in Hobart and really enjoyed it. For some years, she worked in the accounts department and then she became the credit manager. The job really suited her. It mostly involved numbers, and there was always a right and a wrong, which she liked.

Then in 1989, when Birgit was 25, her parents went on a long holiday – a three-month camping trip around Australia. By then, Birgit's two brothers had left the farm, and that meant that Birgit was alone there, caring for all the animals, and the hay paddock, as well as working full-time. While Birgit's mother and father were travelling around Australia, they found a 5-acre block of land for sale in south-eastern New South Wales. It was a lot warmer than their place in Hobart, so Birgit's parents came home, sold their house, bought the block of land, and moved once again. But this time, Birgit did not go with them. She found a flat living by herself in Hobart and then the following year, she was offered a job at the Sheraton hotel, Ayers Rock.

'I loved working at Ayers Rock,' said Birgit. 'It was a great place. I stayed there for two years and I met so many new people. But I'd only been there for about five months when my mother passed away. That's when I started asking questions.'

At the beginning of 1990, Birgit explained, her mother was diagnosed with bowel cancer and died nine months later. Her parents had only recently moved into their new house and they had planned it to be their retirement home. Birgit remembers spending a week with both parents in March 1990, six months before her mother died.

'At that time, my mother kept saying to me that she wouldn't be here for Christmas,' said Birgit, 'and I just ignored her. I hadn't known anyone who had passed away. I blocked it out of my mind that my mother might die. Then, some months later, she had a colostomy and she was back in hospital. My dad phoned to tell me in Ayers Rock. He said, "This is it." I broke down and cried. I booked my flights straight away and flew down and spent time with my mother at the hospital.

'Nobody was coping, though, so I decided that I had to cope. I literally forced myself to cope. Then the actual day that she died I was back at Ayers Rock. I didn't have a phone. I was 26 years old. A friend who had a phone insisted that I give my dad her number so that he could reach me any time. He rang at 5 a.m. that day and my friend came and knocked on my door and told me that my mother had passed away. I cried. But because I had forced myself to cope before, I tried to keep coping.

'I went to the funeral. It was in a church. It was the first time I had ever been in a church, but the person running the service didn't do a lot of God-bothering, so that was good. At that stage I didn't think too much about dying myself, it didn't occur to me, I had to get on with it. Afterwards, I stayed with my father for a week. He was upset and I remember that I couldn't comfort him. I didn't know what to do with him. But once again, I tried to block it out. I tried to get on with it. My mother was dead and so I went back to work and got on with it.'

'Before that time, had you ever thought about whether there was a God?'

'No. It was never really talked about. I knew that my parents didn't like Christians. They were atheists. They wanted to avoid them and so did I. They were anti everything to do with the church. I don't even know why. But they didn't believe in God. I remember one day, the kids at school started talking about going to Sunday school and I wanted to fit in so badly that I asked my parents if I could go to Sunday school. They said it was absolute rubbish. They said it was a money-making thing.'

'Do you think they believed in something else?' I asked.

'No. Actually, at our house, it was almost like my father was the god,' said Birgit. 'He was the man of the house and he had to be revered and obeyed, in everything. I remember that he was given the best food and I was scared of him. So as a teenager I was an angel . . . I was too scared of being hit if I did something wrong. One time, my father bashed me over the head, and my mother and brothers just looked on. That's how it was, all the time. I don't know why they didn't like Christians, or the church.'

'Did you ever own a Bible?'

'When I was younger, I remember that I had a copy of a German storybook Bible and for a while I tried to pray to God at night-time. I'm not exactly sure why I prayed – maybe it was just in case. Then if I prayed at night-time and nothing bad happened the next day, I thought to myself that it was working. God was listening. But not long after that, my family moved house again and I had to share a room with my brother. One night, he heard me whispering prayers and he ridiculed me, so I stopped praying. At first, after I stopped praying, I worried that bad things would happen to me, but then when nothing actually changed, I decided that praying didn't work anyway.'

In 1992, after Birgit's two years in Ayers Rock, she moved to Sydney and found a job in the city. It was there that she met Philip at a singles bar and they married in 1997, when Birgit was 33. Birgit and Philip moved to the south of Sydney. They didn't marry in a church, however, as Birgit was still adamant that she would never have anything to do with the church, ever. In 1998 and 2000, their two daughters were born.

'That was when it changed, slowly,' said Birgit. 'After our children were born, I started to think more about life, and even about dying. I had a lot of questions. What happens when we die? What would happen if I died? Would there be no more of me? How could that be? It worried me a lot. Perhaps it was because of my mother.

'Then when our eldest daughter was in kindergarten, she made one friend, and the two of them were inseparable for a time. They were always going to each other's houses for play dates. I thought it was lovely and I enjoyed meeting the girl's parents and her grandmother. One day, though, I went to their house and I noticed there were lots of God books on their bookshelves. I thought to myself, "Oh no, they're God people." But we didn't talk much about it at the time.

'The following year in July, I saw that the Baptist church had a kids' club in the holidays. There was a sign saying, "Let us entertain your kids for free." I was a busy mum of two children back then – one of them had special needs – so I wasn't going to say no to that! So I sent our eldest daughter to the kids' club and at the end of the day, I went to pick her up. But as I was going inside, I noticed a donation box at the entrance of the church. I thought to myself, "I'm not going to give! It's meant to be free!"

'Then I looked inside the room where the children were. That's when I saw it. Everyone looked so happy – the children and the leaders. I was quite surprised. I didn't expect that. I started to think that maybe something that makes people so happy couldn't be as bad as I'd thought.'

'What happened after that?' I asked.

'Well, for the rest of that year,' said Birgit, 'I didn't think too much about it. I became closer to the girl's mum. Then it was the January holidays and the church put on a kids' club for a whole week. The girl's mum offered to take our daughter every day. So of course I said yes. The two girls went to the kids' club and at the end of the week, the children and parents were invited to the Sunday church service so that we could see what the children had been doing all week. I actually went to a church service! It was the first time I had ever been to a Sunday church service.'

Birgit smiled. 'It actually wasn't that bad,' she said, in a surprised voice. 'My husband and I quite liked it. The people were friendly. I can't remember anything that they said at the service, but it was nice. So after that day we actually started going regularly to the church for a while, for about eighteen months.'

'What did you like about it?' I asked.

'It felt nice to belong to something,' said Birgit. 'They had morning tea every week and we made some friends. I bought a Bible, but I never really looked at it. Nothing stood out. I didn't really learn anything. I had a lot of questions. Mostly, I was still fearful of dying . . . I kept thinking, "One day I'm not going to exist." That was a horrifying thought. I would feel physically sick whenever I thought about it. My time on earth will be finished . . . and there will be no more of me. So we went to church for a while and the people were nice, but I never really understood it. So after a while, we just stopped going. We got out of the habit over time, and we spent Sundays at home.'

Time passed. The children became teenagers. Throughout this time, though, Birgit explained that she had been a gym-goer. She was particularly keen on boxing; she had boxed several times at her local gym in Sutherland. But to box at a gym, you need a partner. The partner holds the bag (or the pads) while you hit the bag, and then you swap. Birgit said she didn't like going to the boxing room without a partner. She explained that it was a bit like going to a dance and sitting in the corner of the room, waiting for someone to ask you to dance – awful. So there was Birgit in June 2012, without a partner and feeling quite intimidated by the group of boxers. As a result, that month she did a lot of circuit classes instead.

After one of the circuit classes, Birgit was leaving the gym and saw that the café was open. She felt like a coffee, but she couldn't see any of her friends from the circuit class. On any other ordinary day, Birgit said, she would have gone home. But then she noticed one friend, sitting with the boxers (mostly men), so she went up to her friend and said, 'Can I join you?' The friend said yes. Birgit sat down with the boxers and they began to talk. One of the men said, 'Didn't you use to box?' Birgit said that she did, but she had stopped boxing because she didn't have a partner. The man said, 'I'll box with you.' His name was Gary. So Birgit and Gary started to box together regularly, at first on a Saturday, and then three times a week. They became boxing partners.

'He was a really easy person to talk to, from the beginning,' said Birgit, 'and we shared some personal stuff. I told him about my mother dying. Early on, I found out that he was an elder in his church. That interested me immediately because I wondered if he could answer some of my questions. It felt like I was still looking for something, and I didn't know what it was. So every week I wanted to ask him about his church, but it was never the right time.'

Then in May 2013, Gary and his wife, Julie, went on an overseas holiday. They were planning to be away for two months. Before they left, Gary said that anyone could follow him on his blog. He was keen for people to make comments, because he wanted to stay in contact with them.

Gary and Julie went to Germany. One day, they visited an old church in a town called Rothenburg ob der Tauber. Birgit had actually been there, as a child. She was interested, so she made a comment on the blog. She asked Gary about church. She said, 'What is it with all these denominations? Don't you all work for the same Boss?'

Gary replied: 'Yes, actually there is one Boss.' He explained that the word itself, though, is a poor human term, because our human bosses work within a framework bound by time – also, our human plans (and our boss's plans) come to nothing when we die. But our Creator God has a plan that is beyond time – before time and matter were formed, outside the barriers of our experience, and sometimes beyond our understanding. Sometimes, said Gary, in our misunderstanding, we try to invent God in our own image.

Birgit wrote back. 'Yes,' she said, 'but don't Jews and Christians and Muslims all worship the same God? And if they do, why don't they agree more?'

Gary said that it was true that Christians read the Old Testament and that Jews and Muslims also hold the Old Testament in high regard. All three faiths say that God is greater than his creation and infinitely greater than anything that we make – which is why we don't find God in buildings. We find him in his Word, the Bible. We don't go to church to be inspired by architecture or art . . . we go to church to increase our knowledge and faith through sharing the Word of God. The Old Testament reveals that God's plan was always to send a mediator, so that we could communicate with God himself, and be made right with him. But when God sent his own Son, Jesus, as the mediator, the Jews refused to accept him as the promised Messiah (or saviour). Jesus was crucified for us, which was amazingly still part of God's plan. The Muslims, on the other hand, accepted Jesus as a prophet and they accepted some of his teachings, but they denied that he was God incarnate on earth. This meant that while we were all 'People of the Book', Jews and Muslims did not have the same promise and assurance of salvation. They were still bound by the same rules and codes of the Torah and the Quran, which were impossible to fulfil because of our sinful, human nature, and therefore deserving of punishment. They still had the same Boss, though, said Gary.

Birgit was interested and Gary kept writing. He mentioned those who were not Jews, or Christians or Muslims – polytheists (who follow many gods), and pantheists (nature worshippers), and agnostics (who are not sure if there is a God) and atheists (who are absolutely sure there is no God). Did they have a Boss? Gary thought that they did. They still had a Boss, he said, they just didn't know him, or acknowledge him. But then . . . it makes one wonder – why did God leave them ignorant of himself? Why would he not just dazzle everyone with miracles until they had to believe?

Gary mentioned a verse from the Gospel of Luke. Jesus was teaching his disciples and he said that many people wouldn't understand his parables. 'The knowledge of the secrets of the kingdom of God has been given to you, but to others I speak in parables, so that, "though seeing, they may not see; though hearing, they may not understand."'[1]

It was hard to understand, said Gary, but maybe the question for all of us is whether we ourselves actually know God, and trust and acknowledge him, as God. Is he *our* Boss?

As soon as Gary and Julie arrived back in Sydney at the end of June, they went to their church and asked their friends to pray for a lady called Birgit who had many questions. But they didn't tell Birgit that. Then Gary went back to the gym. He met Birgit again in the boxing room and he told her that he was writing a sermon on mourning. Gary asked Birgit about her experience after her mother died and how it felt. Birgit told him more of the story.

'The more I talked to Gary,' she said, 'the more I started thinking that I'd like to go to his church and hear him speak, especially about mourning. But I couldn't just turn up there. So I began fishing around for an invitation. I said, "How's your sermon going?" He said, "It's going pretty well." I said, "Good." Then I asked him again. Eventually, he said, "Would you like to come?" I said I thought I might. So Philip and I went to Gary's church that Sunday. But it turned out that the morning before, I'd had news that my favourite uncle had died – my dad's brother, Hilmar. So I was feeling pretty teary . . . and we turned up at Gary's church. It was so different to the other church – it was just a small school hall with a piano, and they sang hymns. I remember walking into the school yard with Phil and saying to him, "We're sitting up the back." But Gary's wife, Julie, who I had never met before, was waiting outside to greet us. She said that she'd saved us seats up the front. OK, I thought, we'll sit up the front. Julie made us feel very welcome and afterwards she introduced us to the minister, Kirk. I cried during the hymns; I didn't even know why I cried. It was good and the sermon was interesting, but overall I still felt like a fish out of water.'

'Did you go again?' I asked.

'Yes,' said Birgit. 'Two weeks later, Gary said that Kirk was preaching an overview of the Bible. It was based on a TV show that I had actually watched . . . I told Gary that the show had really annoyed me and he was interested. He asked me to write a review of the TV show so he could pass it on to Kirk, to maybe use in his sermon. Then he invited us to church. So that Sunday we went to church again. For the first time, the sermon actually made sense! Kirk said the Bible was made up of sixty-six books. He explained the Old Testament and the New Testament, that Jesus was the Son of God, and that he died and rose again so we could belong to him.

'Afterwards, I asked Gary if it would be OK for us to come to church more regularly. I was worried that maybe he wouldn't want me there, in his place. I was just his gym partner and I didn't know if he wanted to mix the two. But he said it was OK, and we had already met Julie, of course, and she was lovely, and he introduced us to other people.'

Not long after that, Kirk invited Birgit and Philip to a special Bible study at their church called 'Christianity Explored'. Gary and Julie were going, as well as one other couple, Sue and Derek. The course lasted for six weeks and they looked at the Gospel of Mark. 'I still didn't get it,' said Birgit. 'Particularly the forgiveness thing. I had so many issues with my father. I didn't know how I could possibly forgive him.

'When I was in my thirties, my father told me that he had never forgiven me for laughing at him when his mother died. I was 4 years old when his mother died! I didn't even know what was going on back then. But my father never forgave me for laughing at him that day . . . So forgiveness was hard. It was a long, slow process. I just didn't understand. I wanted it to be clearer and I wanted to know more. Parts of the Bible seemed really hard for me to understand, like Shakespeare. I never did like Shakespeare! But in that first Bible study I met Sue and we quickly became friends. One day in the holidays, over coffee, I mentioned to her that I found the Bible very hard to read. So she organised a private weekly Bible study with her and another friend called Miriam, on "How to Read the Bible". It was very useful; we became close friends and we did several more of our own Bible studies. But I still had lots of questions.'

'Was there a time when it started to make more sense?' I asked.

'Yes,' said Birgit. 'We attended church every week and I often had questions with regards to a sermon or a Bible study. Something would pop into my mind and I would email Kirk or Gary and they would answer all my questions until I was satisfied. Gary told me that in the first year he had never prayed so much, or researched so much. Bible studies were wonderful. I was welcomed with open arms and they loved my questions and they said that I was like a breath of fresh air. But it was a gradual thing . . .

'One day, I remember, we watched *The Prodigal God* by Timothy Keller. I realised that for all those years, I didn't know what I was looking for. I was just worried about dying. That's when I realised that it was God who was looking for me. I understood forgiveness. I understood what Jesus did. One day after that, I sat up in bed and I just forgave my dad. I told Philip I had decided to forgive him. Carrying a grudge is a waste of time. It freed me. It felt like a weight off my shoulders. I flew to Tasmania to see my dad in his nursing home there. We hadn't spoken for years. By then, he was not well, with Parkinson's disease and Alzheimer's, but we talked together. I visited him twice more that year and it was good. The last visit was the weekend before he died.'

Birgit paused, remembering. We ate some more sushi, with eggplant. Then I asked her how she thought she had changed, having faith in Jesus.

'It feels like I've done a complete 180-degree shift in how I think and behave . . . and how I think about Christians and the church. When I think about dying now, I'm no longer scared. There's no fear, I know that I'm going to be with God. But it's still hard. In fact, I think life is harder as a Christian because now I know what will happen, and I know so many people who don't believe. I go to church on a Sunday and see so many people going about their day and I feel sad for them. I still have questions. I think I will always have questions. Every sermon raises questions and every Bible study raises questions. Maybe that's how it should be. But everyone is so wonderful and patient in answering . . .

'I have these enlightening, wow moments, and then I tell Gary or Julie and they get excited and they want to share it with others. I believe that there is a plan and it's a good plan and I have to trust and pray. But praying is something I'm only just getting the hang of properly. I won't do it out loud in front of anyone, though.

'I do know that God has our time in his hands. It's like Gary said: God is everybody's Boss – but a lot of people don't know that. He has a plan that is beyond time – beyond our understanding . . . I also know that God intervenes all the time, every day.

'I remember another thing,' said Birgit. 'Not long after we started going to church regularly, Phil was in danger of being made redundant. Soon after, his job was reduced to part-time. He worked part-time for eight months and then he was made redundant. After that, he was unemployed for about fourteen months, which was a very difficult time. I remember saying to a few people that ever since we started going to church we'd had nothing but bad luck. The whole church prayed for us every week, though, and they were very supportive. I don't think I would have gotten through it without them. I realised over time that it wasn't actually "bad luck". God had sent us a trial which we survived and we learned from.

'And everything is somehow in God's timing,' she continued. 'Only recently, I was talking to Gary again and he said that he would never normally approach anyone he didn't know to box with him, especially a younger woman. I said that I would never normally join a group for coffee if I didn't know them . . . or admit that I was looking for a boxing partner . . . or tell anyone about my mother . . . or ask if I could go to church. But there we were. The more we talked about it, the more we agreed that it was divine intervention, over time.'

I agreed. 'What's one thing that you would want to say to people now, more than anything?' I asked.

'That it's OK to have questions,' said Birgit. 'Keep asking them . . . and find someone who is willing to answer them. I did. I still am. I call myself a work in progress.'

We both smiled.

7

Broken pieces

Chad – United States of America

Chad and his wife live in a large two-storey house in Denver, Colorado, in the United States. They have two children, two dogs, and they enjoy stunning views of the Rocky Mountains from their windows. It's beautiful, but it hasn't always been that way. Chad grew up in a small farming community in the Midwest state of Iowa. His family were not well-off. By the time Chad was 9 years old, he was working his summer vacations in the soya-bean fields for the local farmers. He was a typical farm boy. Every morning, he would be dropped off in the middle of an 80-acre field, given a 3-foot machete, and told to weed the field by hand. He'd then come home in the evening. It was the 1980s, before pesticides were introduced, and it was very hard work. But as a result, from early on, Chad learned the value of money. By the time he was 16, he was selling cars, mostly illegally . . . and by 21, he had made his first million.

'For all my life,' said Chad, 'I thought money was the answer. I thought it could fix things and that's what I wanted, and needed. My parents weren't farmers, they lived on about 8 acres, and they weren't financially stable. Small-town Iowa was the place of the "haves" and the "have nots". My parents had a very tenuous relationship with each other, predominately due to my father's violent outbursts, and the financial strain. So, from early on, I figured that the only way to make things better was to make money. Making money would equal less stress, which would equal less verbal and physical violence. That seemed liked a simple equation to me.'

When Chad was 5, he was sent to Albert City-Truesdale school. It was a merger between the two towns in Iowa because they didn't have enough children in one town to fill a school. Initially, Chad explained to me over a Skype call, he didn't find school easy or comfortable. He was shy and insecure, and he had a stutter and a lisp, which made public speaking difficult. In the second grade he was sent for a developmental assessment and the teachers decided he needed speech therapy. The teachers also thought he might have a learning disability, so they sent him to complete an IQ test. Surprisingly, the results showed that he had a very high IQ. And everything flipped.

Chad laughed, telling me the story. 'I went from being the kid with the developmental problems who needed extra therapy to suddenly being the kid with the really high IQ who needed extra work. I started doing statistics in fifth grade. I loved mathematics and science. I also loved sport – baseball, basketball, athletics. I was pretty good at it. I was frequently in the local paper. So then the people in the town started putting me on a pedestal. There was so much praise and attention. Back then, in middle Iowa, there wasn't a lot of entertainment – there weren't any movie theatres, or things like that, so people tended to live vicariously through their children (in my opinion), especially if their children were gifted at athletics. For me, the pressure was really on. I loved basketball but it started to define me . . .'

'Did you have any connection with the church while you were growing up?' I asked.

'Yes,' said Chad. 'We grew up in the Methodist church . . . It was small – less than a hundred people. My parents professed to be Christians – they were both Sunday school teachers – and I know they believed in God, but I don't think there was much structure around them to help them walk with God. It was the 1980s in middle Iowa; almost everyone went to church. It was what they all did. It's not the case now. So for me, I went to that church my whole life until I was 16 . . . and that's when I got fed up.'

When they weren't at church, Chad's parents were arguing. 'They were always arguing about money,' he explained. 'They were struggling to keep a roof over our heads, and to feed us. My dad was abusive to my mum. There was a time when I was about 8 years old, and things were out of control at home. My dad picked up his 410 shotgun and he said he was going to shoot all of us – my mum, my brother and I. I don't remember what happened after that. None of us got shot. But it was the typical pattern. He'd get angry, and out of control, and there'd be threats and physical violence. And then we'd go to church . . .

'I know that everyone struggles in this area – matching their behaviour with their beliefs – but the difference was so great at home that it was hard to reconcile. There were also divisions at church – you were either in the rich club or the poor club . . . and we were in the poor club, the ones who were not well regarded. I don't remember hearing the gospel, although I read the Bible, and I could recite all the books in order. But I never read it outside of church. Then, at 16, you have to go through a special class to get confirmed. At that time, we had a legalistic female pastor. It was an anomaly! She was teaching something about slavery. I don't know where she was going with it. My take on it was that she was justifying it – saying that there should be some form of slavery now. I lost it. I got up and walked out of church, thinking, "None of this makes sense." I told my parents I wasn't going back. I was paying my own way by then, making my own decisions, doing my own stuff, buying and selling cars (totally illegally), making my own money. All my problems were solved, right?' Chad smiled. 'I was a good kid, for the most part.'

At the same time, Chad explained that he was being recruited to play basketball at quite a few colleges. His parents couldn't afford to send him to college, but he was being offered sporting scholarships. 'Everyone said, you gotta go to college,' said Chad, 'and I'd figured out that if I wanted to do anything, I had to do it myself. I was lifting weights by then as well, so I was in the best shape of my life. By the time I was 16, I was bigger and stronger than my dad. And that's how I controlled it at home – I protected myself and my mum. But I also knew I had to make money. I didn't want to be like my parents, like how they were at home. For a 16-year-old, I think the pressure was significant, between sports, money and family conflict. There was so much internalised stress. That's when I attempted suicide the first time. I took 400 paracetamol.'

Chad paused, remembering. 'Mental illness was a taboo subject back then,' he said. 'If you went to see a therapist, you wouldn't talk about it. In middle Iowa, the closest psychologist was 140 kilometres away. I did go and see someone and he did the typical thing – gave me medication. But it didn't work. The bigger issue was that they didn't diagnose my bipolar until I was 23. At 16, people just pretended it didn't happen. They wanted it to fade away. They didn't want to talk about it.'

Chad paused again in the story, before continuing, wryly: 'I was a small-town boy who'd been put on a pedestal. It went to my head. And I was alone. I think when you feel alone, you make bad decisions – you act poorly and you lead an unhealthy life. Maybe on the outside we wear the mask of "all is well" but on the inside we're being torn apart. That was me.'

Chad decided to go to Buena Vista University in Iowa to study a double major in business and management information systems, playing basketball at the same time. College was going to be his gateway to the world. As well as studying, he would earn money. Money was what fixed everything. 'I didn't know it then,' he said, 'but I think God was teaching me a lesson. He allowed me to get involved in the satellite TV industry. You see, there were a lot of slaughterhouses in Iowa – cattle, pigs, chickens – and the slaughterhouses began employing the Hispanic community. Back then, the Hispanics were like third-world citizens, but they started to make decent money. Just like anyone, Hispanics watch TV, but there were no Spanish TV programmes on the local cable television stations, although there were three Spanish-speaking channels on satellite TV. So as soon as we introduced satellite TV to the local Hispanic people, it was an instant hit.

'Everyone wanted one for their home. Because of that, the company took off in Iowa, and then it expanded into seven states in America. Soon we had thirty employees, and I was earning a really significant amount of money. Our company name was on the list of the top

100 dealers in the US. I was 21, and I felt rich. I think I actually became the kid who could do no wrong. I was arrogant. The thing with bipolar is that you have a God complex. And, combined with having a high IQ, I started thinking I *was* God. It didn't take too much to get me into trouble. At college, my business lecturers would give us guidance that I thought was not real-world advice, so I would challenge them. Then one of my lecturers kicked me out and gave me an "F". I knew what I was talking about . . . and I was making more money than him – $100,000 a month . . . I was drinking like a fish. So then I just left college, with two subjects to go. I didn't finish my degree. I was arrogant and stupid enough to leave.'

Chad said that he decided to open a second office in Denver. It seemed like a good idea at the time, but it was a melting pot and it was about to explode. 'If I'd not been so arrogant,' he said, 'or if someone had given me some basic advice, it would never have happened. But maybe that was my next lesson from God, although I didn't know it at the time. Our company was part of a distribution model, run by the satellite television company. We were contracted by them, along with 2,000 other "middle men", to help sell and install their equipment and programming across America. So after finding success in Denver (we thought), and after working directly and closely with the satellite television company, suddenly the owner (who is now a billionaire) decided to change the model. He cut the dealers out. It felt like overnight we went out of business. There was no way I could recover, so I lost everything. I went bankrupt . . . I went from living in a 3,000-foot brand-new house to staying in a 300-foot apartment. It wasn't even an apartment. It was a basement. I attempted suicide – I overdosed again.'

This time, Chad explained, he was in a big city, so forty-eight hours later he was taken to Emergency. 'My liver and kidneys were failing,' he said. 'Forty-eight hours is too long. The doctors told me to call my parents – they were basically saying I was going to die. At the time, I was too worried about everyone else – all the people who were going to lose their jobs because of my bankruptcy. I knew I was going from a pedestal to . . . I didn't know what. I had no guidance, no one to talk to, no one to walk me through it. The people I knew either worked for me, or they were just along for the ride.'

Obviously – and incredibly – Chad didn't die. He left the hospital and went to see a psychiatrist. 'It was helpful,' he said, 'because I started to understand bipolar disorder. I started to see why I could do all these things. I thought I was being smarter than everyone else, but actually I was using my bipolar to go longer . . . I was using my disorder to work harder than everyone else.

'Looking back, I don't think I stopped working for twenty years. I pushed myself. I'd go days without sleeping. I just outworked everyone – I did more than them.'

Sometime later, after the bankruptcy, and while Chad was wondering what to do next, one of his ex-employees came to visit him. The man had found a job testing air pollution and he told Chad that his new company needed help. 'He knew I was moping around,' said Chad, 'so he suggested this temporary gig in New Mexico. We had to check out a new plant for a couple of days. I said I'd go with him. We went to Las Vegas and it turned into a big party. But workwise nothing went as planned. The data acquisition system wasn't working. It went on for two weeks. I just wanted to go home. Everyone was standing around not knowing what to do so, eventually, I spoke up. I looked over the boss's shoulder and I told him what was wrong – how to fix it. Within minutes I had it fixed. Everyone wanted to know how I did it, but I just wanted to go home.'

Chad returned home to Denver, but the little interaction had found its way to the owner of the company. The owner called him and said, 'Who are you, and what are you doing in the company?' Then he offered Chad a job – rebuilding their infrastructure and data acquisition systems. Chad took the job, but after a few months of working on that project, he realised that he had finished everything he'd been asked to do. He knew that he could have kept milking the job and taken the owner for a ride, but he didn't want to do that. He'd had experience with employees who treated him that way. So he walked into the owner's office and told him that it was time for him to move on.

'Essentially, I fired myself,' smiled Chad. 'I decided to go into business for myself again. I founded two new companies. One of them was an IT consulting company. I knew I could do that well and charge a lot of money. Money solves all problems! The second company was in mortgages – to help people get mortgages for their homes. I didn't know much about that. I was 23 and I had long hair, so I didn't look the part of a mortgage broker . . . but I liked the model because you could make a lot of money. So the other owner and I started off with a card table, a fax machine and a computer. One of the banks approved me. Once you're approved with one bank, you're approved by lots of them. Then I was back on the pedestal, working like crazy, making a big amount of money, enjoying the party scene. It was the same cycle as before. I'd reinvented myself . . . but inside I was the same . . . and that's when I started getting into heavier drugs – ecstasy, cocaine, marijuana. There were strip clubs. I had no God and no peer group. The people I was with were also using. That's how I spent my twenties. I should have died a couple of times. I don't know how I didn't. The only thing that makes sense to me now is that God was watching over me. I don't think there's any other way I could have survived. He still loved me, even then, in that state of disobedience and self-destruction.'

'Was there a turning point?' I asked.

'Yes,' said Chad. 'I think I had a bit of an awakening in my late twenties. I'd host these parties and I knew I didn't care. It was what life was. I had no relationships. I couldn't date anyone unless she hung out with me and did what I did.

'At the time, I had two people living with me – but I was over it. I asked one of them to leave. He had a girlfriend who was always staying. And then there was Bob. He had a condition known as osteogenesis imperfecta. He stood 3 feet high. He grew up in Wyoming and he'd been to law school, but he smoked a lot of marijuana and he was a raging alcoholic. I tried to help him and to take care of him. But I wanted to get away from his lifestyle. So one day I took Bob aside and I said, "I can't do this anymore . . . We can still be friends but I can't have it in my house." I knew Bob had nowhere else to go. I told him to quit and he did. He did what I said . . . and he died two weeks later.' Chad paused in the story and swallowed. 'I didn't understand the severity of the detox. When he died, it crushed me.'

We both paused and I imagined the guilt and pain. 'I blamed myself,' said Chad. 'I asked him to do it. He tried to quit because I asked him to do it. It's still hard for me to talk about. It was a hard season. None of it was making sense to me. I didn't know what to do. I had no guidance and no medication to manage my bipolar . . . so I decided to leave.

'I'd always wanted to travel and I had a friend who was living in south-east Asia, teaching English as a second language. So my plan was to close both the companies and leave. I would close everything down and move to Thailand to teach English. It took me a year to close down the companies, but I found a place in Phuket that would train me as a TESOL teacher. I don't know what I was thinking – English was not my best thing! But I sold everything I had – my cars, all my possessions.

'It's interesting looking back on it now. Perhaps God was emptying me of all of the material things that I thought solved problems. He does have a funny way of incrementally breaking us down throughout our lives, to bring us closer to him. But I didn't see it that way at the time. I was about to leave. All I had left in my house was my mattress, a TV and a bag of clothes.

'A few days before my house was due to sell, my buddies came over. They knew I was leaving for Thailand, so they wanted to take me out one last time. I didn't want to go. But we went out to a little Irish pub. We were just hanging out. I remember I walked over to get a drink and I looked across the room. There was a girl. She caught my eye and she smiled at me. I had never done this before, but I walked over to talk to her. I asked her if I could buy her a drink. Her name was Beth. She had dark hair and a big smile. We sat together for the next two hours. But it felt like she was ignoring me,' Chad paused in the story and laughed. 'You should talk to Beth about this, though – she remembers it differently to me! But that's how I felt at the time – that she wasn't interested in me. Her friend talked to me more than she did. But what was interesting about that was that in my life, up until that time, no one had ever said no to me. They had always said yes, because I had the money and power. So it was the first time, and if anything, it intrigued me. She was the one that smiled at me, so why wasn't she interested in me?

'But it was a turning point,' explained Chad. 'The next day after that was the first day in my life that I actually had time available. I had no job, no work, no car and no house. So Beth and I hung out together . . . We hung out the next day after that, and the next day after that. We never stopped. On the third day, Beth told me that she played classical violin – she was trained in the Suzuki Method when she was 3 – and she told me that she was a Christian.'

'What did you think when she told you that she was a Christian?' I asked.

'I was OK with it,' said Chad, 'but then that first Sunday, Beth invited me to her church – Applewood Community Church. I went with her. In some ways, it wasn't a big stretch, because I grew up in the church, so going there didn't intimidate me. But I had preconceived notions about what it would be like. The part that Beth didn't tell me was that her dad would be there. When I found out, I was more nervous about that! It turned out that it was a little church, maybe fifty people.

'Part way through the sermon, the pastor stopped and said that we should turn to the person sitting next to us and answer a question. I was sitting next to Beth's dad, and the question was, "What does it mean to be a Christian?" I remember Beth's dad asked me the question first, and I said, "I don't know." I was embarrassed. I really didn't know what it meant. But God was at work in me, again. I knew I was starting to seek something different to what I was doing – that's why I had come up with Thailand. And the church was good. There was a camaraderie there that I hadn't ever seen before. The people seemed to genuinely care for each other. It was Beth's world, so I kept going there, and Beth and I kept hanging out. I remember when I met her mum; her mum said to Beth, "Well, I like him, but you do know how to pick them! He doesn't have a job, a car, a home, and he's moving to Thailand!" It's actually funny for me to think about that now. It's the exact opposite of the equation I had come up with as a kid. Money = stuff, stuff = happiness. I had just met a person who liked me, and I had nothing at all. Even now, when I think of it, I tear up . . . because isn't that God's image? Beth and her church, and the people in it were modelling to me who God is, and what he was like, and how much he loves us.

'But it was true,' went on Chad, 'I didn't have a job, a car, or a home. I delayed going to Thailand. I kept doing what Beth did – I integrated into her life. On the third Sunday at church, the worship pastor cornered me and he said, "Hey, Chad, let's go and have breakfast." Beth was really involved in the worship team, and the guy was like a big brother to Beth, so he was watching out for her. The whole thing seemed like a happier and healthier life than what I'd been living before that. But the next thing that happened was that Beth told me she was going on a short-term mission trip, to Oyacachi in Ecuador, South America. She said there was a team going from her church, and they'd been going there for twenty years. This time, they were going to help build a community centre. I thought I wanted to go too – I liked helping people. And I liked Beth! I thought it would be awesome. But I didn't know what to expect.

'The first night was spent in Quito, the capital of Ecuador, and we were staying in some kind of compound – dormitory-style. We had travelled seventeen hours to get there and we were all settling in, and there was a meal. That's when I met Bruce.'

We both smiled at the mention of Bruce. Darren and I also know Bruce! He lives near us in the Blue Mountains, Australia. He is the reason that I knew about Chad, and could Skype him in Denver. As well as being an extroverted musician and sound engineer, Bruce is fifteen years older than Chad, and a committed Christian.

'I didn't know we were having musicians on the mission trip, from Australia!' laughed Chad. 'But that night Bruce and I got talking, and God started moving in me. I shared parts of my life with Bruce that I hadn't told anyone before. I told him about my suicide attempts and he listened. I got a bit emotional. Then later on, we were all part of a big group in a circle. We had to introduce ourselves to the group and say why we were there in Ecuador. There were some hard stories, and by the time it was my turn, I was a wreck. I told the group about Bob dying. It was still raw, I hadn't processed it well. They all listened to me, and then afterwards Bruce and I talked together, we sang songs, we became buddies. He shared his story with me. We had fun.

'I loved the whole trip – we were in Oyacachi, 25 kilometres from the Amazon jungle – the last stop before the jungle. I was surrounded by American Christians and Ecuadorian Christians – some of them were trying to teach me Quechua – it was awesome to connect with them. Every day we'd have faith-based talks and then we'd have time on our own to journal. God was stirring in me the whole time. I was being softened. It was amazing. I felt closer to the people there than I'd ever felt with people before, and I knew it was because God was part of their life. I also knew I wanted to marry Beth! But I knew I couldn't marry Beth unless I figured out what was happening between me and God.

'Then the trip came to an end, and we were on the way back to Denver, September 2006. Bruce came back to Denver with us too. We were hanging out in Denver for another week, and we talked some more, and it was then that I made my decision to accept Christ. I remember I told everyone about it later in an email . . . which was kind of funny, because I'd spent my whole life on my computer, for work. But I wrote an email to everyone and I made it official. "I'm a Christian", I said, "I've accepted Christ into my heart and asked for forgiveness." And I also said in the email that I loved Beth and I wanted to marry her . . . but I knew that I couldn't love Beth the way she should be loved, before I loved God (not for her, but for me). I told everyone that I'd been reading John 14:21–24 and 1 John 4:7–21, and that's what showed me about the love of God. We only love others because God first loved us.'

'Wow!' I said, enjoying the way God speaks so uniquely into our hearts.

'Yes,' said Chad, 'but at first, I think I expected some big magic lightning bolt that would fix everything in my life. That same week,

I went to see the pastor at our church and I said, "OK, I'm a Christian now, what should I do? What can I be involved in?" But it was a small church and there was no clear group or pathway for new Christians. The pastor asked me if I wanted to start something. I thought, "I'm 30, I've only just become a Christian. And I'm trying *not* to do everything, like I used to do before!" It took me a long time to understand things after that, because early on I didn't have anyone to meet with, or anyone to disciple me. I became a Sunday Christian, but I wasn't consistently reading the Bible. It took a long time for God to work in me.

'Recently I've been reading Matthew 14 – our pastor gave a sermon on it and the message is still shaking my soul. When Jesus fed the 5,000 people, they "all ate and were satisfied", and it was amazing. Afterwards it says "the disciples picked up twelve basketfuls of broken pieces that were left over". The leftovers are important to the story, but it's the phrase that interests me – the "broken pieces". Now I realise there were broken pieces in my life – there still are, and there always will be. We're not in heaven yet, and I will keep working on the broken pieces for the rest of my life. But I didn't know that at the time.'

In the next four years after Chad's trip to Equador, he said that he married Beth, bought a house, started two more companies, and they had two children. "It was the same sort of pattern," he admitted. "I was a professing Christian, but I didn't have the building blocks of a healthy faith, or relationship with God. I needed discipling, and I didn't really have anyone to do that. Bruce was in Australia, on the other side of the world. Beth was involved in the praise and worship team at church, so she was OK for a time, she was plugged in . . . but then she had our first daughter, Avery, and she lost that connection.

'We had no idea what we were doing as parents. We didn't know anyone else with newborn kids. I loved being a dad, but Avery was the first baby I had ever held. It was hard for Beth. She went into postpartum depression. We had no family near us at the time. It was a new kind of darkness. I didn't know if we were going to make it . . . and I didn't think it was supposed to be like that, now that I was a

Christian. So I did what I always do . . . I started a new company! I thought, "I'm a husband now, I've got kids, I have to make money and I have to make sure everyone is looked after. A new company will make it better."

'It didn't, of course,' Chad continued. 'It was a lot of hours. I was working like crazy again – unbalanced and unhealthy – and I wasn't invested in my relationship with God at all. Things were hard, so after a while, we moved churches, and that was good for Beth. She became involved in a mum's programme and that really helped her. She didn't feel alone anymore. And she got back involved in praise and worship. But I still wasn't plugged in. I didn't have the flexibility in my day that Beth had.

'I was back in company-building mode. Eventually, all of my past came back into play. I have this way of getting caught up in things. That same year, my dad died of cancer, and he didn't leave his affairs in order at all. He didn't leave my mum in a good situation financially, and my brother wasn't able to contribute any financial support. He had problems of his own. So I had to step in and help my mum. I went into fix-it mode again. I didn't get to mourn my dad. I tried to sort out their mess. That went on for a long time – years.'

We both paused, thinking about the pattern. 'I think it really only changed four years ago,' said Chad. 'Beth and I moved churches again and one of the pastors invited us to join a weekly Bible study group, with five or six other couples. I'd never been in a small group before. I'm not good at small talk, so I felt intimidated by it, sick to the stomach. But we went along to the group. They were doing a Bible study on marriage and relationships. By the third week, I was break-ing down in tears, explaining my story. That was the beginning of my closer walk with Jesus. It was still bumpy, of course, but God just kept pulling me closer, and I kept pressing in. We got really close to the other couples. Beth and I did a lot of the hosting, and there was a group leader who was biblically very well-read. Before that time, I was the guy who carried Beth's violin for her, but 2013 was the year when I got more plugged in to the community. It was really good, it was much better, but I was still not reading the Bible regularly by myself.'

'What happened with work?' I asked.

'Well, I was still working all the time,' said Chad. 'One of the companies I was involved in became one of the fastest-growing supplement companies in the US. The amount of time I was putting into it was crazy – I was slowly killing myself. Physically, mentally and emotionally I was expending energy into the companies and not into my relationship with God, or my family. Then late last year, my right-hand man in one of the businesses left. I was crushed. I had 300 people between the two companies, who I felt were dependent on me. I didn't know what to do. I was a wreck. I still hadn't dealt with the broken pieces, although I could see God at work around me. I was really just putting on layers of Christian veneer.

'Beth could see what was happening to me. So at the beginning of this year, 2017, I crashed. I had a psychotic episode . . . and I walked away. I booked myself into a hotel room for three days, by myself, out of contact with everyone. That was my final awakening. I realised that my habits were killing me – the amount of time I spent on my phone, online, in meetings for work, all the time. I went to the doctor and he said, "If you don't figure this out, you're going to kill yourself." Everything was too high – my blood pressure, my cholesterol, everything.

'The last seven months have been better,' he went on. 'I've focused on my spiritual health and my physical health and my relational health. It's been a lot better – our marriage and family and church. I've dropped 30 pounds, and I've been reading the Bible almost every day by myself – from the front to the back. That's made the difference. I don't use notes, I just read it – one or two chapters a day. I've been meeting with my pastor, and some of the older Christian guys at church for mentoring. Beth and I have been going to marriage counselling. That should be compulsory! Everybody should do it.' Chad paused. 'I'm transitioning, you could say. God's timing is impeccable, of course . . . During this same season, our senior pastors are changing and they are launching more men's ministry events, a growth track programme and much more. It's a great testament to God having the right things for you, at the right time, in the right place.'

I agreed with him. 'What have you learned more than anything, in your faith journey?' I asked.

'Money is *not* the answer,' smiled Chad. 'It doesn't matter if I have seven billion dollars, or seven dollars. What matters is my one-on-one relationship with God. It's the only answer. The simplest thing I can be, and the best thing I can be, is a child of God. And I can be part of the Christian community, I can serve the community. I *have* to be part of it. It's the long relationships with others that matter – the discipleship. I still think that if someone had said that to me years ago – if they'd just said, "You're not alone" – when I thought I had to do it by myself, then maybe that would have helped me. I've realised now that I'm not really in control of very much. I'm not God! For forty-one years I tried to control everything, and now I see that I can just make choices with the opportunities that God puts in front of me. I'm getting better at listening to him – hearing what he wants me to do, versus what I want to do.'

'Do you have a specific idea about what he wants you to do next?' I queried.

'I have some ideas,' smiled Chad. 'I've realised that I have a large network of people, and I could use that network to glorify God, versus make money. Those people around me also have reach – they have access to millions of people through various online strategies. It's a mostly secular reach but I wonder if I could use that for good reasons – use my tendencies for the gospel, especially in mentoring and discipling other Christians. For me, I think that if someone had just walked me through what it meant to be a Christian, early on, or the process of finding God, that would have been helpful.

'It's a difficult thing for everyone to know how to be a Christian, and it can take a long time to figure out. In all of the companies I've been a part of, it's always about getting a person to take the next step, to get them to *do* something, to take action, stay focused, make a decision. Of course, it was usually to buy something. However, the principles seem to align with discipleship. Someone who walks alongside a new Christian ultimately encourages that person to do all the same things, right? Maybe we need to learn how to do that better in the faith-based world. So I wonder how I could work on something that would guide and direct people in their journey with God – not control them, but rather help God serve up information, and people, and content, at the right time, in the right way, with all of the technology he has allowed to be built.

'These days, people spend on average six hours a day on their devices, on top of their work. But we don't spend that much time in the Bible, or being a disciple, so how could we use that, and change that? If we're going to expand the kingdom, I think we have to go to where the people are, and figure out how to do that. Of course, I don't agree with everything that devices are being used for, and I know for a fact that most of it is not for God, but God would not have allowed them to be created if he hadn't wanted us to do something about it. Think about it,' said Chad, 'as human beings, have we ever had a time in our existence when we could communicate with the masses as fast as we can today? It only gets faster and more far-reaching every day. What if we used those systems – the internet, smart phones, tablets and computers – to spread the gospel in a united way, a true Christian faith-based way – helping people on their journey to him, guiding them, nurturing them, holding them accountable? Online marketers are doing this every day, but it's 99 per cent about selling you something. What if we served up God in every interaction with these platforms? Imagine what could be accomplished for his kingdom then! That's what I'm thinking about at the moment.'

Chad paused and smiled. 'I tend to think big . . . but I'm learning to live small and let God handle the big stuff. I'm sure he will let me know, at the right time, in the right way, and put the right people in my path to work on this idea, if it's his. But for now, I'm focused on the men's group chilli cook-off, in two weeks' time at church. Those relationships are just as important as the *big idea*. No big idea ever works without a lot of little steps, and the stronger and more intentional each step is, the better the foundation is for the big stuff.'

We both agreed, but at this point in the Skype call, Chad was in his car and he explained that he had just parked outside a coffee shop. It was 7.30 a.m. in Denver (and past midnight in Australia). We'd been talking since 5.30 a.m., his time. 'I'm sorry,' he said, really quickly, 'but I gotta go. I'm meeting with one of my pastors from my church right now, and we'll pray together and talk about my ideas. I'm not sure what God has in store for us, but I'm excited to find out . . .'

'OK, great, thanks!' I said. 'I hope it goes well.'

Then I turned off my Skype, and prayed for Chad, feeling amazed again that God uses everything in our lives, and our stories, for his good, ongoing purposes – even the broken pieces.

8

The wrong shape

Cathy – Australia

Darren and I have known Cathy and her husband, Rod, for nearly twenty years. Cathy is the chaplain at Nepean Hospital in western Sydney, a gourmet cook, a pastoral care trainer, a board member for Thorndale Foundation,[1] a loved and involved wife, mother and grandmother, a maker of extraordinary quilts, a deeply encouraging friend . . . and she's lived with a significant disability for all of her life.

Cathy was born in Australia in 1961. It was the same year that a polio vaccine was developed worldwide and came into commercial use in Australia, in an oral form. Back then, the vaccine was given to babies at 6 months old. When Cathy was 5 months old, though, she became very sick overnight. By the time her parents checked her in the morning, Cathy was unconscious. They quickly sent one of her older brothers across the road to call an ambulance, on the public phone. The ambulance arrived and took Cathy straight to the children's hospital at Camperdown (a suburb of Sydney) where she was diagnosed with polio and put in an isolation room. So the polio vaccine due to be given at 6 months old was four weeks too late for Cathy.

Cathy was the fifth of seven children, and her family lived in a very small fibro-cement house in Lalor Park, western Sydney. There wasn't very much money to go around. Cathy's father was an inter-state truck driver and her mother was a barmaid.

'We lived in a housing commission house,' said Cathy. 'The boys slept in the garage. From time to time other families would come and stay with us too. Mum and Dad were always helping out needy people. But they bought everything on time-payment and I remember the man from the department store coming to the front door. He would want to know where the money was, but Mum would hear him coming, and she would hide somewhere and tell us to say that she wasn't at home. It was week-to-week survival.'

For the first three years of her life, though, Cathy did not live at home. She stayed in the hospital until her third birthday. After the initial polio infection died down, the doctors discovered that Cathy's entire left leg and left side were paralysed, and her right side was partially paralysed. As a result of the paralysis, Cathy's respiratory system was compromised. She needed ongoing attention and treatment.

'How did that work out with your family?' I asked. 'Did they visit you in hospital?'

'It was very hard on them,' said Cathy. 'They had to look after all the other kids, and they were working full-time, and they lived a long way away from Camperdown . . . so they would come to the hospital on Sundays, and stay for an hour. That was all. Then, not long after that, my father had a cancer diagnosis and my mother got hepatitis. It was very hard.'

Before I could ask any more questions about how Cathy survived in hospital on her own for three years, she described being sent home from hospital. At the age of 3 she was given two long-leg iron calipers, a leather corset around her trunk and four iron bars holding her neck in place. She was also given crutches and taught how to swing her legs through, slowly and painfully. She could move very short distances.

'I didn't wear the calipers all the time at home,' said Cathy. 'In the house, I'd take them off and I'd drag myself around on the floor, on my bottom, or with my arms. I was always on the ground. I got quite good at it. My mum said that I was determined.'

Not long after Cathy came home from the hospital, she was sent to Northcott School for Crippled Children, in Sydney. Cathy explained that a car would pick her up every morning and then do the rounds, picking up the other kids. 'It was wonderful,' she said. 'It felt like everyone was the same . . . Some of the other kids had spina bifida, cerebral palsy, or muscular dystrophy. They'd give us "flithers" to play on – they were little seats with three wheels and we'd move them with our arms. For the first time, I was mobile, and fast! We didn't do much actual schoolwork, but we felt like we fitted in.'

But then, when Cathy was 7 years old, she was moved to the local public school. Her parents decided that Cathy needed a normal upbringing and that segregation wasn't the best thing for her. In the future, they said, she would have to fit into a walking world, so she would need to learn how to cope. 'I hated it,' said Cathy. 'I begged, every day, to be taken back to Northcott.'

'What was the worst part of it?' I asked.

'Everybody else could run around,' she said. 'They'd all be in the playground, playing, throwing balls at each other, and every day I'd be sitting by myself, against the brick wall, with my crutches and my calipers, wishing that someone would throw the ball to me. Nobody ever did. Even at home, it was the same. All my six brothers and sisters were always outside, playing down the street with their friends . . . I'd be sitting at home, on the back steps.' She paused, and I tried to imagine the 7-year-old Cathy, alone on a concrete step. 'I couldn't move very much,' she said. 'I didn't have a wheelchair until I was in my twenties, so I couldn't go out and, all the time, I felt like I wasn't a whole person. I was deformed and separate. I was the wrong shape, always.'

We both drank more tea and Cathy shifted herself in her wheelchair to breathe more easily and keep talking. She then described the next three years at the local public school, where she continued to attend but couldn't join in. When she was 10, the doctors decided that she needed a spinal fusion; it was meant to take six months but took two years, so she spent that time in hospital. It was the first time the operation had been done in Australia.

'Actually, those two years were easier,' said Cathy. 'It was a re-lief. In hospital, I fitted in. *Everybody* was lying on a bed, and life in an institution was what I knew. It was almost like I was back at Northcott.' She smiled. 'There was a real freedom. I didn't have my parents telling me what to do anymore.'

There were many setbacks, and during that entire time, Cathy was lying flat on her back – except when she was hanging from the ceiling by skull prongs as the medical staff re-did her body plasters and tried to straighten her spine. Screws in her head attached to long irons held the body plaster in place. I asked Cathy what that was like.

'Well,' she said, 'I remember the days they'd come and tighten the screws in my head. They'd say to me, "This won't hurt." Then I'd go ballistic. I pulled their hair and I scratched their faces. After that, they thought they'd give me a sedative. Every day, I'd watch the clock, waiting for the next pain relief. I'd beg the nurses for something for the pain, but they weren't allowed to give it a minute before the time.'

'What did you do during those years, as well as watching the clock?' I asked.

'I was lying completely flat on my back,' said Cathy, 'but they put a mirror above me. So if they put something on my chest, like a book, I could see it. But I couldn't read very well at that point, and what little I could read, I had to read in mirror image. Apart from that, a few of the other patients and I caused havoc. We'd try to nick cigarettes and light them under the sheets, or we'd steal a nurse's starched cap and we'd throw it to someone else in a wheelchair and they'd run it under the water – that sort of thing. Then the nurse would get into trouble from the matron, and there would be havoc.' We both smiled.

Cathy explained that after she was discharged from the hospital, she spent another year at Northcott. 'By then,' she said, 'I was a master of manipulation. I'd have a pressing need to go to see the physiotherapist, which would get me out of class, and then I'd con myself a wheelchair, and I'd do laps around the place. My teacher was so easy to wrap around my finger. As well as that, the teachers were busy. They'd have to traipse us around the countryside to tug on people's heartstrings, so the school could get extra funding. But we got a hot lunch every day, and that was good, and hot chocolate at morning tea. We were spoilt.'

'At this point,' I said, 'what did you know about Jesus?'

'Nothing at all,' said Cathy. 'I'd never heard of him. I'd never met a Christian in my life or anyone with any faith. I'd never been to church or to Sunday school.'

'Your parents had no religious background?' I asked.

'None at all,' said Cathy. 'They were just trying to survive.'

In 1973, Cathy was 12 years old and the school at Northcott sent a group of the children to Camp Howard in the Blue Mountains for the weekend. 'It was a Christian camp,' said Cathy. 'Up until then, as I said, I'd never heard about Jesus. I remember that we played games at the camp and the first thing I noticed was that the leaders were lovely people. They were all young and it felt like they cared about us. They talked to us – and there was a speaker. He got up one day and he said that Jesus died for us, and he wants to be our friend. He said that Jesus is standing at the door, knocking, and if any of us hears his voice and opens the door, he'll come in and eat with us.[2]

'It amazed me,' said Cathy, smiling. 'I'd been pretty short on friends up until that time. I didn't have any. There were people I met in the hospital, but they were older than me, and after I left the hospital I never saw them again. Everyone else at school wanted to play in the traditional way, which I couldn't. So when the speaker said that Jesus would come and live in my heart and be my friend, I said yes straight away . . . I'd be happy for anyone to be my friend. I thought he would probably get bored, though, and he wouldn't stay very long, like everyone else, but it sounded good. So I prayed the "sinner's prayer" and then we went home from the camp. Two weeks later, two of the leaders from camp came to visit me, and they gave me a Bible. I still have it here, forty-four years later.'

'Did you read it back then?' I queried.

'I couldn't read very well at the time,' said Cathy, 'but I looked at it, and I started going to church. My mum dropped me off each week. She probably thought it was a good idea that I join in something, anything. But it was hard for a while at church. I still felt separate; I sat up the back and nobody really spoke to me; they were probably scared. It was a different era . . .

'After a while, I met some Christian girls through Girl Guides and they took me to their church and their youth group. That was when I really started to understand the gospel. I understood what Jesus had done for me. It all made sense to me then.'

'Was there something in particular that stood out?' I asked.

'The promise of heaven,' said Cathy, straight away. 'The Bible says that we've been made right with God through Jesus now, and there's a time coming when we're going to be made whole. I'd never heard of heaven before and it seemed like an unimaginable gift at the time. I felt so separate and deformed, I didn't fit in, I was the wrong shape . . . and I remember hearing that there will be a time when Jesus will return and I will be made whole. I understood it. I knew it was absolutely true. Now, when I look back, I can see God's timing. He knew that the next few years after that would be really hard and I needed to hold onto that promise.'

When Cathy turned 13, her parents sent her to the local Blacktown Girls High School. It was 1974 and back then, schools were not renowned for their disability access or commitment to equal opportunities. There were stairs everywhere.

'I did have some friends from youth group at the school,' said Cathy, 'and they were helpful, but I still felt like I was the outsider . . . I was the only person who couldn't walk. I couldn't get to my classes. So at 14 years and 9 months, I left school for good. It was as soon as I could leave. I still felt like I was the wrong shape, and I would never find a place to fit.'

After leaving school, Cathy said that she went to a business school in Parramatta, west of Sydney. She learned typing and accountancy work. Not long after the course, her parents decided to move out of Sydney. They told Cathy about their decision, and they said that she would need to find her own accommodation from then on, because they were leaving. Cathy was 15.

She remembers spending some time in a rundown shack in Toongabbie, Sydney, and a period with her older brother, and another time with a family from church. It went on for a while, and then she finished her course and got a job with a real estate agent.

But the job was supported employment and it only lasted for three months. The authorities told Cathy that she should go on a disability pension. Cathy refused. She was 16. So they told her to go and stay at a rehabilitation centre called Mount Wilga, in Hornsby.

'I wasn't sure what they were rehabilitating me *from*, or *to*, but I went anyway,' said Cathy. 'I didn't have a lot of options and I needed a place to live, so I did what I was told. I started to see that God has his plans. At Mount Wilga, there were several Christians, also being rehabilitated, and we became friends. One of them had severe injuries from a car accident and the others were paraplegics and quadriplegics. They were really struggling with their losses. When I spent time with them, I realised that I didn't feel the same kind of loss that they did. I was different. I'd always been like this, it was all that I knew. It actually made me think about who I was, and that maybe I was OK.

'We went to church and youth group together. One Friday night one of my friends was back in the hospital, having an operation, and so we went to visit her. Her able-bodied friend was also there and he offered to drive us all home. His name was Rod. We said yes, that would be good, but only if he would take us to youth group on the way. He agreed to do that, and he came with us to youth group. He probably thought he'd been dropped onto another planet. He said he normally went to the pub on Friday nights. But after youth group, Rod drove me home and we talked all night about everything. I liked him, but I never thought I'd see him again.'

Three days later, Rod knocked at Cathy's door and he asked her out for a drink. He suggested that they go to a nice place up the street.

'I was so surprised,' said Cathy. 'Mostly that he showed up . . . and I said yes without thinking. But when he suggested the place up the street, I didn't know if I could walk that far. I don't think Rod realised that I couldn't walk. So we started off – I had my calipers and my crutches – and I thought I was going to die. I'd never walked that far in my life. I was 17.' Cathy smiled. 'We've seen each other every day since then. Now I'm 56. All my friends back then wanted to know how I got him. He was so good-looking. I told them that I didn't know. We were married when I was 19. I was working at the Teacher's Federation, and we moved to a house on a hill in the Blue Mountains, with thirteen steps. It was the denial period of my life. And then we had Andy.'

I smiled, watching her. 'Tell me about the thirteen steps, and Andy.'

'It was crazy,' said Cathy. 'The land we bought was on a hill in the Blue Mountains, but Rod thought we could manage. So we built a house with thirteen steps in it. I had a wheelchair in the car, but nothing for inside, so I'd use my calipers and crutches or Rod would carry me in and out of the house. That was OK if we left the house at the same time. But then when I had Andy, it was very hard. I'd crawl across the floor with him, pulling him on a blanket beside me. I had a terrible fear of dropping him. Then he started school and I stopped working so I could take him to school. But I had to go in and out of the house by myself. Awful.'

'What did you do?' I asked.

'I told Rod that we would have to move out,' said Cathy, 'or *I* would move out. I couldn't live there anymore. Eventually he agreed and we bought a house in Mount Riverview with a ramp.'

'Did you go to church during that time?' I queried.

'No,' said Cathy. 'I didn't want to risk things with Rod. I was still as surprised as everyone else that he was actually my husband. So I had insisted that we were married by a minister, but after that we didn't have contact with a church. Before we met, Rod told me that he had read the whole Bible and he had an intellectual point of view about God. He acknowledged God as a creator, but it meant nothing to him personally. So we would have long intellectual debates about it, but we didn't go to church.

'For me, I knew God and I still talked to him. I also knew that giving birth to a healthy baby was a miracle that only God could have performed, and I was so thankful for him. Until the day Andy was born, the doctors thought he would be sick. So I was really thankful for Andy and when he was 18 months old, I had a strong sense that I needed to go back to church. I wanted to honour God for the gift he had given me, in Andy. That's when I started going to the local Presbyterian church; Rod came with me occasionally. Then we both started doing Bible study with the minister.

'All his life Rod had struggled with the concept of a loving father. He'd had a pretty tough dad. Then over time, he started to like the minister. The minister was an older man, and he became like a father figure to Rod. Rod started to see that the minister was like he was, a lovely man, because he reflected his heavenly Father. That's when Rod came to faith in Jesus.'

I smiled. 'How was it for you . . . that sense that you described before of not being the right shape, or of not fitting in?'

'I still felt it, all the time,' said Cathy. 'But I think, at first, I got busy. I tried to hide it. When I was working for the Teacher's Federation, I started in the mailroom. It had been another supported employment position and I knew I would have to work harder than everyone else to keep the job after the initial three months. There were five other people employed with me but I was the only one to be kept on. I worked there for the next six years, and I moved through to becoming the pay mistress, and then soon I was almost running the place. I did the same thing at church. I had six positions at one time. I think it was my Superhero period – I was trying to make up for what was wrong with me. I was trying to fill the hole that was my wrong shape. Maybe I was trying to make it up to God, or make sure he didn't walk out on me. I wanted to keep him in my heart. So I thought I'd have to serve him really well if I was going to do that. We'd have women's events at the church and I'd end up doing all the cooking . . .'

I smiled at that point. It was true. When I first met Cathy, it was 1998, and we were both attending the same local Presbyterian church. Back then, Cathy was in her late thirties, and I was in my early thirties. We'd both show up at these social events. I'd arrive late, in a fluster, with our three small boys, and Cathy would be in the middle of everything, in her wheelchair, producing and serving the most amazing food – gourmet salads and desserts and roast dinners for 100 people, from her wheelchair. That's not an exaggeration. At first I wondered how she did it. I myself had worked in rehabilitation as a physiotherapist, so I knew how hard it was to function in a wheelchair. But Cathy seemed so capable that after a while I stopped thinking about it, or even noticing her wheelchair. I think everyone else did the same. We'd just turn up and find out that Cathy was in charge, and then we'd all relax, knowing everything would be fine!

Cathy agreed with my observation. 'Yes,' she said. 'That's exactly how it was . . . except that for me, the sense of being "broken", or of missing something, of not being able to play . . . was present well into my adult life, even at all those events. I was always the wrong shape. So I kept busy and I worked hard, maybe thinking that if I had that "something", or if I worked hard, then I'd be a better mother, or a better wife, or even a better Christian. God would love me more. I knew the gospel, I believed it, I knew about grace and forgiveness, but I was trying to work hard and figure out what it meant, day-to-day, in my life. From the day I gave my life to Christ, I knew I would be made perfect in heaven, but I was trying to work out how to live here, and how to survive within this brokenness. I thought perhaps being busy, or serving as much as I could, was the answer.'

When Cathy was 42, she said the answers shifted. She decided to retrain as a hospital chaplain. 'Up until then,' she said, 'I'd been working for the Teacher's Federation, and then on the switchboard, and then as an office manager for a plumbing company, and it was good, but at 42, I decided I wanted to do something that would use my gifts in pastoral care and encouragement. I thought I could be a hospital chaplain. I knew about medical institutions! But the problem was that I had finished school when I was 14. I'd never been to university, or studied anything, so I didn't know if I could do it.'

Cathy enrolled in a hospital chaplaincy course. The first problem was that the course was in a multi-storey building with no lifts. It wasn't wheelchair-accessible at all. There were stairs everywhere, just like at Blacktown Girls High School. The toilets were downstairs on a different level to the classrooms. Cathy had to go back to using her calipers and crutches for the entire six months, somehow levering herself up the stairs, multiple times a day. It was very painful and difficult. She developed sores on her legs and she wanted to give up. Then one day at the course, the lesson required the students to read a passage from John 5. It was about the man by the pool at Bethesda.

He'd been an invalid for thirty-eight years. Jesus saw him lying there and said, 'Do you want to get well?'

Cathy read the passage and thought, 'What a strange question. Does he want to be well? Of course he wants to be well! Why would Jesus ask that? He's been waiting there for thirty-eight years!' But then Cathy started to wonder if the man *was* getting something out of being unwell. She paused in her reading. 'I felt like I needed to ask myself that same question,' she said. 'Do I want to be well? And what does it mean for me to be well? Can I be well in my wheelchair?'

Cathy knew she couldn't walk and she would never be able to walk. But could she be well? And what would that mean? As she talked to me about being well, I wondered what it meant, for all of us. So I asked her what she thought.

'I realised after a while,' said Cathy, 'that being well meant I could live a full life. And a full life meant being able to use my gifts . . . not necessarily being able to walk. For me, being well meant being comfortable with who I was . . . with the fact that I couldn't walk. It meant believing that I am no less of a person because I can't walk. It meant not blaming myself for my shape. It was a turning point for me. After the course, I decided I would put away my crutches and calipers for good, and stop trying to walk – stop trying to do something I couldn't do. I was 42 years old and I moved into my wheelchair permanently. I had to be comfortable and complete and accept the shape that I was.'

After the chaplaincy course, Cathy said that she got a job as the hospital chaplain at Nepean Hospital, in western Sydney. It's a 520-bed hospital that serves 54,000 patients per year. Cathy was given a certain number of wards to look after and patients to visit. On the first day at work, she found her way around the hospital in her wheelchair and began by visiting a lady on the orthopaedic ward. The lady had recently had her right leg amputated. She saw Cathy coming towards her in her wheelchair and she immediately opened up to her. The lady cried and told Cathy everything about feeling broken and the wrong shape and never fitting in. Cathy understood. She was able to share her faith.

'It has happened like that every day since then, for fourteen years,' said Cathy. 'They talk to me. They see me and they know I'll understand. We share and pray and talk about Jesus. Now, finally, after all these years, I'm starting to see why I am this shape. It's not a wrong shape. It's a different shape. And it has purpose and meaning for the place I am now. I can even help other people to be comfortable with their shape. I can show them that they're OK.'

Another day, Cathy visited a man who had been in hospital for months. He was in pain, unable to eat. He was very thin and his pacemaker was poking through his chest. He sat on his hospital bed in despair. He asked Cathy where God was in all of this. Cathy nodded and said, 'Yes . . . it's pretty hard to see God in all of this. I get how hard it is. But if we take God out of the picture, where do we go from here? We'd still be dying, and we'd have no hope.' The man and Cathy kept talking and they began to share the promises of God – the truth that Jesus forgives us and gives us life. When this life is over, there's more to come. That's what we hold on to.

'But actually,' said Cathy, 'the best thing for me has been spending time in the mental health ward. That's where I've learned the most. There are often up to thirty-seven patients on the ward, and many of them are there because they can't find a reason to live. They tell me their stories and it's heartbreaking. Every Monday morning we run a chapel service there. We sing "Amazing Grace" and they cry. Some of them go to sleep. They say it's the only time they feel at peace, and they can actually relax. Many of them have been returning to the ward a lot over the years for readmissions, so I know them really well, and they know me . . . and over time, I've had this sense that we're the same, but different. I'm broken and they're broken, in different ways. We all need hope, and we want hope.

'One day, I was wheeling through the ward and a lady called out to me. "You're beautiful," she said. I stopped . . . She said to me . . . "You're beautiful! There's something in your eyes." It meant something to me that day. They know me. They see something different. We share together. And I hope they see something more of Jesus.

'Another day on the ward, a man said he wished that I could walk. He wanted me to walk and he felt sad for me that I couldn't walk and

I was in this wheelchair. So I explained to him that I would never be able to walk, but I would dance with him in heaven, and he said he was looking forward to that.

'I think actually people see me in this chair and they have an immediate sense that I understand suffering, so they talk to me. They know my suffering isn't the same as theirs, but it's shared. Because I've shared suffering, they also listen to me when we share Jesus. So perhaps the biggest thing I've had to learn is that God has made me to be who he needs me to be . . . in this shape, in this chair.'

'Is it still hard sometimes?' I asked.

'Yes, it's still hard sometimes . . .' said Cathy, 'to not live life like . . . the little girl in the playground who couldn't play. I know I'm not that girl anymore, but for a long time I thought I was. I lived like I was missing out on something, or there was something missing in me . . . Actually, when I was little,' Cathy smiled, 'I used to throw away the screws on my crutches . . . into the bushes. I'd call my dad and I'd tell him my crutches were broken and he'd have to take a day off work to fix them. We'd go to the hardware store together to get them fixed. I'd get what I wanted – time alone with my dad. I think I have to be careful of still doing that.'

'Isn't that OK, though, sometimes?' I asked. 'If people want to help you?'

'Yes, sometimes it's OK,' admitted Cathy. 'People want to help me and that's nice. But say, for example, I'm at work, at the hospital. I'd love someone to get me a cup of tea, because it's pretty hard for me to carry boiling water in a cup, in this wheelchair. Sometimes that's nice, if someone brings me a cup of tea . . . but the grown-up Cathy has to work out how to get the tea from the tea room and back to the office, without spilling it. So now, I use an extra big cup and I fill it up half way, and then it doesn't spill. I can get myself a cup of tea, as a grown-up.

'But yes, for all of us, it's tempting, occasionally, to act out the victim. Some time ago, I was writing an essay for my course and it was hard. Essays aren't my thing. At the same time, I started to get pains in my chest. I knew it was my scoliosis. But the thought crossed my mind, briefly. "I could go to emergency and mention chest pain and I'd get attention. My friends would come. They'd bring me food.""

Cathy smiled. 'But I actually want real relationships and to not be the dependent little girl anymore. I've had to work through that. One day, I actually wrote a letter to my younger self – the little girl in the playground. I said thank you to her – because a lot of what happened in the playground made me who I am today. But I also said that I was going to leave her in the playground, where she was.'

'And what would you say now, about the biggest thing you've learned, as a Christian?' I questioned.

'I'm a different shape,' said Cathy. 'I'm unusual but I'm the way God wants me to be. He's planted me where he wants me. So I have to choose to accept that and live that out, rather than throw the screws away and get attention. It's not easy, though. It's a process. Sometimes it's easy to obsess about disability and put everything that's broken onto that. Or in an opposite way, we can get so caught up in the striving for perfection, that we can't feel OK with the way we are. Sometimes we all want to shake our fist at God. There's nothing fair about getting polio at 5 months old. I think God is OK with that. We don't have to pretend. We can shake our fists at him . . . But we also have a choice – to not live out of that unfairness, and to not be the victim. So every day . . . I have to get in the car and go to the hospital and make the cup of tea and keep on going.' She paused. 'And I have to notice what God is doing now, today. I have to remember the story isn't over. When I first heard about Jesus when I was 12 years old, I was amazed that God loved me and that he promised me life forever. I was his. And I have held on to the promise all these years . . . that one day he will make me whole.'

Cathy smiled at me. 'I still think about heaven a lot,' she said. 'When I get there, I know the first thing I'm going to do is say to Jesus, "Hang on a minute, Jesus, I'll be back soon. I just have to run down the stairs.""

I smiled with her, imagining my dear friend in full flight, running down the stairs.

9

It was the way they prayed

Hama – northern Iraq

In April 2009 Darren and I spent two weeks in the Kurdish area of northern Iraq. We stayed with our friends Hama and Kathie, who were living in their two-storey apartment in Sulaymaniyah, a city 340 kilometres north of Baghdad. Hama explained to us early on that he grew up in Sulaymaniyah in the 1960s. Back then, the city was small. There were horses and carts in the streets. Hama and his friends used to play soccer in the graveyard opposite his house. They'd play every day with a plastic ball, and often it cracked. Every time the ball would crack, they'd fill it up with scrunched paper, and keep playing. It was all that they had.

Hama said that his father was born in one of the nearby villages, and came to Sulaymaniyah in the 1950s to try to find work as a labourer on the mud roofs. Then later, Hama's father found a job as a mechanic and he began to drive trucks. After some time, he met a nice village girl, and they had ten children. Three of the children died when they were small. Hama was the middle child. He doesn't know the date that he was born. I wondered how that could be. 'Do you have any idea of the year?' I asked.

'No,' said Hama. 'It could be 1961, or 1962, or even 1963.' He paused. 'My parents are illiterate, so they couldn't write down the date. Lots of older people in Sulaymaniyah are like that. I was born at home, so there was nobody else around to write down the date.'

'Did they have to register the birth back then?' I asked.

'No,' he said. 'They had to register a child when he or she went to school, but that was five or six years later, so nobody could remember the date the child was born, or even the year. Some people try to remember an incident that happened in the same year that a child was born – maybe there was a fight or a battle or a flood or a storm. For me, my mum said there was a battle in Bazian (the region around Sulaymaniyah) the year I was born. That was when the Iraqi army fought with the Kurds, which was in 1962, so maybe that was when I was born.'

'Being Kurdish,' I said, 'did your parents practise the Muslim faith?'

'Back then, and even now,' said Hama, 'if you're born a Muslim, you're a Muslim, even without praying, or practising . . . My father didn't pray or practise anything, but my mother did. She prayed to Allah every day by rote, memorising the prayers in Arabic. She didn't speak Arabic or understand it at all. She couldn't read anything, in any language. She spoke Kurdish, so she didn't understand the Arabic that she prayed, but she kept praying it. It seemed like a ritual to me. And there was pressure among the women. They would socialise together, meeting in their houses, so there was pressure on her to pray and follow the rituals. Every day, my mother would kneel on the ground in the morning, before sunrise, and then five times through the day, praying the Quran. But she didn't know what she was praying, and she didn't wear a hijab. She wore the *jilli kurdi*. That's the traditional Kurdish dress, with a headscarf, and beads around the waist. She even wore it in bed.'

'What did you think, yourself, as you watched your mother pray?' I queried.

'I knew that she didn't understand what she was praying,' said Hama. 'I could understand Arabic. I went to the local school and we learned Arabic in Year 4. We had instruction in the Quran twice a week. We had to write exams on the Quran and we had to go to the mosque, as part of religious instruction . . . so I knew what my mother was saying, and she didn't. I thought it was a ritual for her. Back then, Zoroastrian belief was also practised – the religion of our ancestors. It seemed fake to me. It seemed like words, or an outward behaviour, not coming from their hearts, and I didn't follow it. My family didn't force me . . .'

'Did you ever hear about Jesus as a child?' I asked.

'I have a vague memory,' said Hama, 'that once I was sitting at home. There were five of us children by then and our parents. We were living in one room, with a flat mud roof. We had mattresses on the floor and a kerosene burner in the corner. I was sitting with my older brother and he was reading a religious book from school. It was about Jesus. He said something to me about Jesus dying and then rising from the dead. When I heard that, I wanted to know more about Jesus. I didn't know how Jesus died, so I pictured him hanging from a beam of a mud roof like ours. It was all I knew. But the image stuck with me . . . and the name of Jesus. Then there was another day later, when I was a teenager, I was working as a labourer and one of the jobs was to fix a Christian church. Being at the church brought back the memory of the name of Jesus. It was a good memory. I believe God put it on my mind. But it was all that I knew. There was no other information.'

'During that time, as you were growing up,' I said, 'was there a question you had about life, or about yourself, or a longing for something?'

'I feared Allah,' said Hama. 'I thought there was something to be afraid of, and that he was watching. If I did something wrong, even if no one else was watching, I thought that Allah was . . . He might punish me. But there was a war on all of the time. It was normal. We hadn't had a day's peace in northern Iraq for hundreds of years. We didn't even know what it was. It felt like there was no way out, and no end to the fighting and at the time, no end to Saddam Hussein's regime.[1] Everybody was afraid of him. Even if they got rid of Saddam, he had sons. We felt like nobody could do anything.'

During our visit with Hama and Kathie in Sulaymaniyah, they showed us around the city and the markets, and they fed us delicious Kurdish food. One day, they took us to the old town of Erbil to meet their friends, and we walked inside an old tomb, dated 200 BC.

Then another day we met the local Iraqi physiotherapists and we saw the three hospitals in Sulaymaniyah. But the most heartbreaking moment was when we went to see the museum, located a block away from Hama and Kathie's apartment. It was the site where Saddam Hussein had held his headquarters in 1991. Inside the museum, there was an entire area of mirrored glass. Each of the 182,000 tiny pieces of mirrored glass fragments stuck to the walls represented the 182,000 people who had died during the attacks in 1991. In that year, around 4,500 Kurdish towns were destroyed by Saddam Hussein and his forces. In the next room, there were photos – faces of the people who had died. As we walked past them, Hama pointed to each of them and he told us their names. They were his friends, his teachers and his neighbours.

Later, back at Hama and Kathie's house, we were standing by their window and Hama said that, for as long as he could remember, they had never painted their houses. There was no point, he said. There could be bullets through them. 'In all my life,' said Hama, 'I can't remember a day's peace.'

Hama explained that when he was a boy in the 1960s and early 1970s, he would watch the Iraqi army walk through the streets of Sulaymaniyah and grab the young men and take them away. One day in particular, it was 3 o'clock in the afternoon and Hama saw an army jeep chasing three men through the street to capture them. Hama knew that they would all be shot or put in prison. The men never came back. Another day, the army nearly captured Hama's father, but just at that moment, Hama's sister started screaming. She was nearby and she could see what was happening. So, after a while, the men released Hama's father.

'My father came home that day,' said Hama, 'but the memory hasn't gone away. Even now, in Iraq, there are mothers who are still crying for their sons, and their husbands. They've never been found. As a boy, I didn't want that to happen to my mother. I would have done anything to make sure she didn't cry . . .'

In 1982, Hama said, he finished school and went to Mosul University to study physics. It was the middle of the Iran-Iraq war.

The law back then said that anyone who was over 18 and who was not studying would be required to join the Iraqi army, so Hama studied. In July 1987 he finished his physics degree, but the war was still continuing. Fortunately for Hama, his ID card said that he was officially a student until 1988, so for the next six months he helped to build a house. Then it was 1988 and Hama had to be much more careful, in order not to be found and recruited into the army. He didn't want to be someone who disappeared and caused his mother to cry, so he went into hiding and avoided the checkpoints.

But then, in August 1988, the war between Iran and Iraq came to an end. It was officially over. Both Iran and Iraq agreed to UN-established peace terms. A million people had died in the conflict but the war was officially over. Some people relaxed. Saddam Hussein announced publicly that he would forgive the Kurdish men who had not joined the army and, as part of that forgiveness, Saddam invited all the young men into his office, to have their names officially cleared. So Hama went into the office. He wanted to be free to walk around outside, without fear of recruitment. But while Hama was at the office, an announcement was made that all the young men standing in the office had to get on a bus.

'It was a trick,' said Hama. 'They took us in a bus to a town called Diwaniyah, 186 kilometres south of Baghdad. Then when we got there, they divided us into two groups and they kept us there for two and a half months, in training. After that, they released us, but they had a plan. Saddam was increasing the size of his army so that he could invade Kuwait. He was in debt to Kuwait and Saudi Arabia. And Kuwait was oil-rich. So, immediately after they released us, they called us back up into the army. They had us by then and Saddam was very powerful. He had a million soldiers in Iraq. There was nowhere to run. Even if we had tried to leave Sulaymaniyah, we wouldn't have been able to get past the Ring Road. Like now, the Ring Road surrounded the city, and if we'd ventured past it, we would have been shot immediately.'

We could see the Ring Road from where we sat in Hama and Kathie's house, listening to the story. We paused; I was trying to imagine it.

Then Hama explained that he obeyed orders and travelled south again to Hillah, the old Babylonian city, an hour out of Baghdad. He was trained in artillery, mainly because he had studied mathematics and physics. After six months of training, Saddam Hussein was ready to invade the oil-rich Kuwait. Hama's group travelled south-east. It was September 1990. Hama was worried.

'In the army, you're meant to wear a chain around your neck,' he said, 'with a metal plate on it. It's identification for when you die. Everybody has their name punched into the metal. But because we were Kurdish, we didn't have a metal plate. I didn't know what to do. What would happen if I died? Nobody would know who I was . . . so I found an old metal plate that belonged to someone else. I wrote my name on a piece of paper and I taped it onto the metal plate. But it was just paper. If I died, the paper would be destroyed and my mother would never be told. She would spend the rest of her life crying . . . and I couldn't bear that.'

Hama said his troop was given orders to move south. It was a hot day and there were quite a few of them in the van. Hama was meant to be tracking the route. Then someone suggested that they stop the van by the river and go for a swim. Hama looked out of the window and he saw the opportunity. Everybody else was getting out of the van and walking down the slope to swim in the river. Hama decided that if he ran, he would be ahead of them. They would take a while to climb up the slope and go after him. So Hama picked up his bag, jumped out of the van, and he began to walk away, quickly. He left his gun and binoculars in the van. All he had in his bag was a loaf of bread and some dates. Hama walked as quickly as he could to the nearest small town and then he headed for Baghdad.

'I got to Baghdad,' he said, 'and I caught a bus home to Sulaymaniyah. I tried to avoid the check points. I was really worried. I was still wearing my army clothes, so on the bus I made up a story, in case someone asked me where I was going. But nobody asked me anything.'

Hama said that he arrived in Sulaymaniyah and went back into hiding for many months. By then, there was a rumour that the Iraqi army were searching house to house for people who had escaped from the army. 'My neighbour had also escaped,' said Hama. 'So he and I dug a hole in our back garden. It was big enough for us both to sit in it. We put a tray of soil over the top of us and we used some plant material as camouflage.'

I stared at Hama, imagining him and his neighbour hiding in a hole in his garden for months.

'We didn't hide in it for the whole time,' he explained. 'We had the hole ready to hide in. The rest of the time we hid in the house. We never left the house. We were so afraid of being captured. One night, the army came looking for us, and that was when my neighbour and I spent the night in the hole.'

'They didn't find you?'

'No,' said Hama.

'And what happened to your troop that went south to Kuwait?'

'I don't know. I never heard from them,' said Hama. 'If I'd stayed, I might be dead.'

Six and a half months after the Iraqi troops invaded Kuwait, in late February 1991, Hama said that the UN forces, led by the US, gave Saddam Hussein an ultimatum to withdraw. Two days after that, the ultimatum was ignored, and the Gulf War began. The US-led forces began extensive bombing of the Iraqi military installations as well as strategic targets in Baghdad. The bombing was devastating and the Iraqi army was crippled, so their troops retreated.

'At that point, Bush thought it was over,' said Hama. 'He thought Saddam was out. Even the Iraqi people were rising up against Saddam and his army. There were demonstrations in the streets and Bush must have thought that was a good thing. But then Saddam complained to President Bush that he couldn't retreat his troops if the bridges were destroyed and if transport was impossible. He said he needed helicopters to move his troops, so he asked President Bush for permission to use helicopters as transport. Bush gave him permission to use the helicopters, and an agreement was signed. Saddam then manned the helicopters and he began shooting at us, at Iraqi civilians, from the sky.

'They had guns in the helicopters,' said Hama, 'and they began attacking our people. Everybody started to run. We could hear the gunfire from where we were, here in Sulaymaniyah. There were tanks surrounding the city and there were bombs going off. We knew the gunfire was 25 kilometres away. People started shouting, "Run towards the mountain!" Everybody was running. Some of them even made it as far as Iran. But everyone was heading north, towards the mountains. There were 2 million Kurds on that road over there, fleeing towards the mountains.'

Hama paused and he pointed at the road north of their house. It led up into the mountains. The four of us had travelled on it the day before on our way to a picnic. 'That's the road where we fled,' he said. 'Two million of us. I was with my mother and father and two of my sisters. I was carrying a blanket and some bread. We were walking. Then the army started shooting at us from their helicopters. There was a tractor in front of me. A cap flew off from the water heater and the boiling water blew up in my face . . . My face was burned. I covered myself in my scarf. Then, immediately in front of me, I saw bullets land on an open truck. The truck was carrying women and children. I saw a mother cradling her baby. Then I saw the baby's head blown off, in the mother's arms, straight in front of me. I can't begin to tell you what I saw. Terrible things happened. The baby's face was gone, and the mother was screaming, but the truck kept driving up the hill. It couldn't stop. It kept going, driving up that hill . . .'

At that point, we cried. We stopped the story. It was all too hard. We made sweet Kurdish tea and ate soft Iraqi dates and we cried some more. I stared out of the window at the mountain north of Hama's house. How does he look at it, every day?

Later, we asked Hama what happened next. Hama said that he and his family made it into the mountains and they stayed there for three weeks. They were cold and hungry. There was snow. The Red Cross began distributing tents and blankets, and then they brought in food – rice and flour and cheese. Hama's family found the remains of a bombed-out house in the destroyed village of Penjwen and they stayed there on the mountain. The Red Cross left after a few weeks and handed over their work to Medair, an international non-governmental organisation (NGO). There were millions of refugees. Hama stayed on and volunteered to help Medair. He began serving with them, mostly doing translation and cooking. Soon, he became a field officer.

'One day,' he said, 'everything changed. I met the camp manager. He was a Kurdish man. He was sitting in front of his tent, in the camp, and I saw that he had a Bible in his hands, in Arabic. He was reading it. I saw it and, straight away, I asked him if I could borrow it. He said yes and he gave it to me.'

Hama then described beginning to read the Bible for the first time, on the mountain, surrounded by tents and snow and refugees. 'I'd wanted to read about Jesus for a long time,' he said. 'Ever since I was a child and I heard his name, I'd been looking for something to read about Jesus and I'd never been able to find anything, even at university. Nobody knew anything about Jesus. I still had that memory from when I was a child – the name of Jesus. So I started reading the Bible.'

'Where did you start?' I asked.

'I started with the Gospel of Matthew,' said Hama. 'I remember reading up to chapter 6. And in chapter 6 it said that when you pray, don't be like the hypocrites. Don't show off on the street corners, or pretend, or use long, complicated words that you don't understand. Just "go into your room, close the door and pray to your Father", who knows what you need.[2] He'll listen to you. Then it says how to pray. It says to ask for forgiveness and for help. It says we have been forgiven. It all made sense to me. That's what Jesus was talking about. Don't show off or pretend. Don't do things out of ritual, or because other people are watching you, or telling you to do them. Your heavenly Father knows what you need. He's listening to you. You can talk to him. It was quiet and humble.

'It felt like everything that I was looking for was on those pages. And everything I didn't like about the Muslim faith was also there. In Islam, when you give, most people want other people to see. But in the Gospel of Matthew it says when you give, "do not let your left hand know what your right hand is doing".[3] Do it in secret. It was enough. I sat there on the mountain, surrounded by tents and snow and refugees and I kept reading. I didn't understand everything about Jesus' death and resurrection, but I kept reading and I understood it later.

'I read that Jesus died on a cross, not hung from a beam on a mud roof of a Kurdish house,' Hama smiled. 'But it was the praying that made sense to me first.'

Soon, Hama began to join with the Christians in Medair to read the Bible with them. He noticed that when they prayed out loud it sounded different. It wasn't like Muslim prayers. The Christians didn't stand up and bow down or repeat the same thing, over and over again. They didn't pretend or show off. They just spoke from their hearts. It felt new, and there seemed to be peace for Hama, for the first time.

'Soon I began to pray myself,' said Hama, 'in my heart and some-times out loud. I joined in the group, and I worshipped in English. I got peace in my heart . . . I never had it before. I didn't feel like I was wasting my time. I knew that God was listening. I knew that what Jesus said was good. Then I heard about the whole Bible. They used storytelling, starting with Moses. It fitted together, but it was a process. It wasn't a sudden vision.'

After about six months, Hama said that he met Kathie. She was a young Australian physiotherapist, who had previously worked for many years in Turkey, and had recently joined the Medair team there in Penjwen, northern Iraq. Hama and Kathie began to talk and go to Bible study together. They kept working for the same organisation and they were married in May 1995.

'What did your parents think?' I asked.

'My parents didn't say very much,' said Hama, 'because they loved us so much. They had only one issue – the age difference. Kathie is four years older than me.

'In the early 1990s, it was still a dangerous time in Iraqi Kurdistan. Even after we left Penjwen, Saddam Hussein was still alive and well, and he was sending gunmen into the liberated Kurdish areas to at-tack foreigners. So we always had armed bodyguards with us, and we checked for car bombs and we travelled in convoys whenever we went anywhere.

'I remember there was one time in April 1994 . . . an armed guard and I escorted Kathie and another foreigner up to Erbil to join a convoy heading to the Turkish border. We said goodbye to them and then we were on our way back down to Sulaymaniyah. We were on an isolated, hilly section of the road, and I saw a small car parked near the top of the hill with a man holding out an empty jerrycan. As our diesel pick-up approached, two gunmen sprang up from behind the parked car and they opened fire at us. Bullets were hitting our car, my bodyguard ducked his head down and I kept driving, though I knew I'd been shot.

'Once we'd passed the gunmen, my bodyguard immediately returned fire through the rear window. Over the crest of the hill I was able to stop the vehicle. My bodyguard continued to shoot at the three attackers who were running away over the fields. I managed to crawl away from our vehicle and off the road. I thought I was going to die and I prayed to God to forgive me even though I hadn't been baptised. I'd been reading the Bible and I was deeply moved by Jesus' words about forgiveness. I knew that if someone followed Jesus they should be baptised.

'Meanwhile, back on the roadside, the next vehicle to come along the road was another foreign NGO vehicle, and they were able to radio our office in Sulaymaniyah and alert the team that we were being driven straight to the Emergency Hospital. The next few days were a blur of anaesthetic recovery and pain. I had been shot in my shoulder and upper leg, but miraculously the bullets had not hit any major blood vessel, nerve or bone, and my bodyguard just had a graze across the back of his head where a bullet had taken the skin off. Both of us knew that God had spared our lives. Later, when the vehicle was brought back to our office, we counted thirteen bullet holes piercing the front, driver's side and rear panels of the vehicle. Shortly after being shot, I was baptised in Jesus' name.'

At around about that time, explained Hama, a small group of Christians who worked with Medair's Emergency Response team in Penjwen decided to continue helping in Iraqi Kurdistan, even though most of the other organisations were withdrawing. The Gulf War humanitarian disaster had passed, but the Kurdish leaders were still welcoming foreigners to provide aid, so with help from friends in the Netherlands, this small group of Christians registered a new organisation called ACORN – A Community Oriented Rehabilitation Network. Their prime purpose was to establish a medical rehabilitation programme for disabled children. When they arrived in Sulaymaniyah, their team leader asked Hama if he would like to work with them. Apparently, they needed someone to set up their first office, find houses for expatriate staff to live in, and to employ local drivers, cooks and bodyguards. Hama said yes, he would like to do that. Over time, he also helped to set up a temporary clinic, and then renovated the old buildings chosen by the health department for the new service, contracted builders and painters, and was responsible for logistics, purchasing, staff rosters and payroll.

'I enjoyed my work,' said Hama, 'and the Christian foreigners kept praying together and singing songs of thanks to God. They were honestly helping the children with disabilities and they cared for their families. So I continued to work with ACORN in building regional physiotherapy clinics and in various management roles until 2009.'

'And how do you think it changed you, being a Christian?' I asked.

'My life changed a lot after knowing Jesus,' said Hama. 'I could talk to God. Before, I didn't know who to talk to, and I had lots of fear when I was doing something wrong. I was always punishing myself and I didn't know there was a God who died for my sin so I could be free . . . That's how I've changed. I can pray to God now.'

Not long after Darren and I visited Iraq in 2009, Hama and Kathie moved permanently to Australia to help care for Kathie's elderly parents. When they arrived, they put their two children in local Australian schools, and Hama tried to find work locally. It was a bit sporadic, but they were comfortable. There was hot water in the taps and there were no bullet holes in their walls. We met up with them occasionally and shared meals with them. One day in particular, the four of us were visiting a local church in western Sydney. It was 2014 and, once again, there was war in Iraq, with ISIS. The pastor of the local church stopped his sermon and he suggested that we break into small groups and pray for Iraq. Of course, the pastor didn't realise that Hama was in the room. So we moved into a small group with Hama and we prayed for Iraq. I was feeling particularly wordless, overwhelmed by the situation. But Hama knew how to pray, quietly from his heart. He prayed for all of them, in ISIS, in Syria and Iraq – the Christians, the Sunnis, the Shi'ites, everybody. He prayed for a long time that everyone would know the truth of the God who loves them and who has given them peace through his Son. Afterwards, I thought about how much more it meant, coming from him.

Two years later, in 2016, Hama went back to northern Iraq for six months, to help. By then, ISIS were very strong in the area and they were trying to gain ground. Hama worked with two of his friends who had set up an organisation supporting street children and refugees. They helped the children to work through their trauma by playing. Hama also assisted with building projects at the refugee camps, and he spent time with his extended family and met his friends at the bazaar.

'It's very hard,' he said to us later, when he returned to Australia. 'The hardest thing is feeling like I can't help very much from here. Or I can't even get people to understand the Kurdish situation. I'd like to go back permanently to Iraq, to live and to help, but we need to be here for now for Kathie's mother. She is very old – and our son has special needs. So in the meantime, I stay here and I pray for my people and I try to get people to understand.'

The Kurdish situation *is* difficult to understand and it has gone on for generations. Hama and Kathie have tried to explain it to us – that the Kurds are the largest ethnic group in the world without their own independent land. There are apparently more than 40 million Kurds, living in parts of Turkey, Iran, northern Iraq, Syria and Armenia. The land they inhabit is also a passageway, so anyone travelling south from Russia, or east from Greece, or west from anywhere in the Middle East, needs to pass through Kurdish land. That means that everybody wants to control the passageway. Even Alexander the Great passed through Kurdish land in 330 BC. Over the centuries the Kurds have been oppressed by Turkey, Iran, Iraq and now ISIS. For the Kurds, and for half a million refugees from Syria, it's still the middle of the story. As I write this, the Kurds are voting for independence.

'We're all in the middle of the story,' said Hama, 'and it's hard. But looking back on my life, I see some things more clearly. I know that I've changed. I grew up being afraid of everything. There were so many things to be afraid of. There was war all of the time. I didn't want to disappear and cause my mother to cry. Even now, I still carry fear in my everyday life. I still feel afraid of authority. Maybe it's wired in me. At the moment, I'm studying for an exam . . . in electrical engineering, and I feel afraid. But I know that there is no fear in my walk with God. The memory of Jesus stuck with me. Then, when I was on the mountain, it was the practice of the Christians. They were different. They were humble when they prayed, and they helped people. I said that I used to fear God, but I didn't know who he was back then. Then I found him, or he found me, and I knew him. I wanted to follow him. Now I don't feel afraid when I am in church or when I read the Bible. That's the difference.

'I still think that Matthew 6 is the answer. It's our hearts that matter, not the outward show. I can't explain it better than that, but I know that it's in my heart.'

At this point, Hama handed us some more dates. They were Iraqi, all the way from Sulaymaniyah, and they were very soft. As we ate them, we thought again of the pain, and the answers, that Hama had found on the mountain.

We prayed, quietly.

10

I was always curious

Angelina – Australia and Turkey

I first met Angelina in July 2017 at a friend's house. She was living in Sydney, in a single room, after having been in Turkey for twenty-three years. Our friends told me that I should speak with her. 'She's got a great story,' they said, 'and she'll enjoy telling it to you. She used to follow the New Age movement, and she became a Christian later in life.'

'Great,' I thought, 'that sounds interesting.' So the next time I visited our friends, I popped in to see Angelina.

She had silver hair and deep brown eyes. She was 86 years old. Inside her single room there was a bed with a floral bedspread in one corner, a fridge, a kettle, a cupboard, a desk, and two black office chairs. Angelina herself sat on one of the office chairs and she invited me to sit on the other one. Then she offered me lemon and ginger tea with honey, and I looked at her pictures while the kettle boiled. Angelina's Bible lay on her bed, alongside an iPad in a sparkling green cover. She explained that she was born in Sydney on 24 May 1931, during the Great Depression. Her parents had little work and no money, so the family moved regularly, from one place to another, while her father lined up for work at the Balmain docks, waiting to clean the boats or do simple repairs.

'Everyone was looking for work back then,' said Angelina. 'My father was a seaman by trade and he would occasionally catch the tram from Balmain to the Sydney markets to find leftover food. Then afterwards, he would bring the food home for us and get off the tram before it was time to pay the tram fare.'

Angelina's parents were Italian by background, and Catholic, so Angelina was sent to the local Catholic primary school – St Augustine's, Balmain and then later she went to St Benedict's, Broadway. Back then, though, Italians weren't popular and Angelina was picked on at school. 'I was very dark,' she explained, 'which is why they picked on me. And my parents weren't actually religious. They didn't go to church regularly, only at Christmas and Easter . . . although sometimes they would call out to Jesus if they needed help.'

The family needed help often, but never more so than when Angelina was 5 years old. Her only sibling, an older brother named Mickey, died of rheumatic heart failure. 'He was my best friend,' said Angelina, quietly. 'He was 7 years old – eighteen months older than me. The doctors thought he had growing pains and they sent him home without treatment. By the time they realised it was heart disease, it was too late. Mickey died, and the grief went inside of me. I became very quiet. I grew up on my own, after that.'

A few years later, Angelina said that she started going to Mass by herself every Sunday. The family didn't go to Mass, but because she was at a Catholic school, the teachers expected her to attend. So off she went by herself – every Sunday morning, sometimes as early as 6 a.m. if she needed to do something else that day. 'I didn't like the sermon or the religious stuff,' she said. 'It seemed like all talk and little substance. But I would always turn up in time for communion. I was devoted to communion.'

I paused in the story, wondering why a child, or even an early teenager, would be devoted to communion. Angelina caught my eye. 'I don't know,' she said. 'I think it was the Holy Spirit. I can't explain it any other way. But communion seemed like the most important thing, so I wanted to go to Mass and take communion.'

I nodded, still wondering, and Angelina kept going with the story. 'Back then, though,' she said, 'I was always trying to be good. I could never be good. I remember I was always confessing something. We had to go to confession in those days. I was very aware of the habitual things I did all the time that were wrong and I would confess them to the priest and then I'd feel better for a while. Then I'd sin again. It was a relief to get it all off my chest. Back then, we were meant to go to confession at least once a year, and if I hadn't been for a while, I'd feel desperate to go. But even when I went, it felt binding, it didn't release me.'

When Angelina was 11, she said she was confirmed in the Catholic Church. She remembers kneeling at the front of the church by the altar and making a promise. 'Everyone had to promise something,' she said, 'so I promised that I wouldn't drink alcohol until I was 21.' Angelina paused, smiling. 'I don't even know why I promised that. Maybe it was suggested to me.'

Angelina finished school in 1945 when she was 14. 'There weren't many options back then,' she said. 'My family couldn't afford to send me to university, but there was a college at school where I could learn shorthand and typing, so I did that. I learned to be a stenographer and then I got a job at the Forestry Commission, in an old building in the city, on the corner of Margaret and York streets.'

'Did you like it?' I asked, trying to picture a 15-year-old Angelina, with the deep brown eyes, typing all day.

'No,' said Angelina. 'It was very boring. But I stayed at the Forestry Commission until I got married. I got married in 1954. My mum was always keen for me to find a boy, but I was too quiet to talk to anyone. I was shy, ever since my brother died, so my mum kept looking and she found me a cute boy at the butcher's. He was a rascal, but it didn't matter to me. I fell in love with him, and then we were married.'

Between them, Angelina and her new husband had £210, so they bought a block of land at Woy Woy, on the Central Coast. Angelina's husband was especially fond of fishing, so the location suited them. Later, they sold the block of land and bought a small house at Ettalong. During this time, Angelina's husband opened his own butcher's shop, and they had five children, born between 1954 and 1966.

'He was very good while he wasn't drinking,' explained Angelina. 'He was a benevolent person. But we didn't have a lot in common. He had his mates, and his sport, and the sports club. We both had baggage. He wasn't interested in church. I tried to keep going to church for a while, but it wasn't easy. It was out of obligation, not out of love for God, so I stopped going and I stopped praying. And he began to drink more.'

In 1971, Angelina turned 40. By then, her husband was regularly staying out all night, and Angelina knew that he was seeing someone else. One night she felt sure that things were coming to a head, and she remembers falling on the floor, distressed and crying. As she cried, a psalm and a prayer came to her mind. She hadn't heard it spoken for at least twenty years. 'Come Holy Spirit, fill the hearts of your faithful. And kindle in them the fire of your love. Send forth your Spirit and they shall be created. And you will renew the face of the earth.'[1] The prayer was based on Psalm 104, verse 30, from the King James Version of the Bible. That night, Angelina repeated the prayer over and over again, on the floor, until she felt spent and exhausted and finally went to bed.

'Do you wonder why that particular verse came to mind?' I asked.

'No,' said Angelina. 'I think it was a prayer that I'd said so often . . . but not for years. That night, I couldn't stop saying it – over and over again. Then my husband left me a few weeks later. He came to the house while I was out shopping. He packed all of his belongings and he took the car, and left me a note and $40.'

At the time, Angelina's children were aged 5, 10, 12, 15 and 17. The youngest was about to start school. 'I grieved for six months,' she said. 'I shut myself in my room . . . I felt abandoned. I didn't want to come out . . . and then after six months, I knew I had to come out. I had to survive and provide for my children. I hadn't worked for seventeen years, but my mother said that she knew someone who organised jewellery parties and she asked me if I would like to become a salesperson. I said I would. So I had a party at home, and I found that I was quite good at sales. It was a surprise.

'Back then, I didn't have a car, so I went by tram and bus and train all over the city, running jewellery parties. I was very successful. After a while, my mother said that I should get a car. So I bought a big, old Ford with only six months of life left in it . . . I went everywhere in that car, all around the country. Then I was promoted. I had staff under me. I even bought a new car. I was able to provide for my children, and other people helped me. But emotionally, I was empty, all of the time. I still felt abandoned. I had very little left to give to the children. I know that they struggled.'

'Did you ever wonder again about the psalm that you prayed?' I asked.

'No,' said Angelina. 'Not for another seventeen years. I didn't think about it, or believe in Jesus. Instead, I became fascinated by other things – wicked practices.'

After seven years, Angelina explained that the business was doing well and she had found a new freedom in her life. Her divorce also came through around that time. She paused.

'Freedom is a good and wonderful thing,' she said, slowly, 'but with it comes choice. We can choose so that it benefits us, or we can choose so that it destroys us. The next part of my life was a result of the choices I made.'

Angelina became what she now calls a New Age gypsy. In 1978 she sold her house and bought into a guesthouse in the Upper Blue Mountains with friends who were also involved in the New Age movement. 'My friends were mostly a peaceful lot,' she said. 'They loved each other. They wanted peace . . . but of course, they had no moral compass at all. I also lost my moral compass. It began when I went to yoga classes to help with my arthritis, and then I became involved. I'd always been interested in Eastern religions. There was a spirit of fascination, and it drew me in. I had no conscience about it at all. I began to read everything I could, including books written by the followers of the Ascended Masters.'

When Angelina tried to tell me about the Ascended Masters, I had no idea what she was talking about. I found out later, on Google, that Ascended Masters are people believed to be spiritually enlightened beings. They were apparently ordinary humans in previous incarnations, but then went through a series of six spiritual transformations, which made them capable of dwelling on the sixth dimension . . . and therefore Ascended Masters.[2] I decided I need to ask Angelina about the dimensions.

'We live in a four-dimensional world,' said Angelina. 'But there are actually ten known dimensions and the other dimensions are in the spiritual realm. Of course, we aren't capable of living there, but the followers of the Ascended Masters are trying to get there. The sixth dimension is a state we find within ourselves. People who practise New Age believe that we are all incarnations of the presence. There is no god. We find it within. We become god. And they think that Jesus is one of the Masters, but he is not the final Master.'

Angelina said that she spent the next ten years, travelling around the countryside in her car, camping out with her friends, occasionally under the stars. 'I was so deceived,' she said. 'But I wanted more and more of the forbidden fruit and I was never satisfied. There were so many avenues to go down. I heard about a lady called Peace Pilgrim. She used to travel across America and proclaim peace everywhere. She never used soap. I thought, "Well, that sounds interesting." So I started travelling to Queensland and back. It was what everyone was doing at the time – camping in the parks, or staying in the homes of other New Age followers. There was music and dancing – the power was in the sound, everyone chanting "Om" together, like a motor. It was captivating. But underneath, it was very dark, and there was a lot of damage . . . and I did terrible things.' Angelina paused. 'The people believe that you are your own god . . . which means you can reach a level of self-sufficiency through meditation and visiting the gurus. There were screeds of books to read . . .

'In deep meditation, there are all kinds of demons involved. And there was a lot of sexual sin – although it wasn't always revealed. There was a façade. I would say that it was OK, but I was never satisfied. I always wanted something more. Everyone wanted something. Really, I was like a pig in mud, happily swimming along in a sea of sewage. I was filthy. In truth, it was bondage to the devil, but I didn't see it then.'

On Angelina's final journey, she said, she was on her way to Perth from Sydney, and she had never been to Perth before. But when she arrived in Victoria, she noticed something different. 'Everywhere I went,' she said, 'the doors seemed shut. I thought I'd call on my friends from the New Age, but the people who had previously been welcoming to me were not answering their doors, or their phones. I wondered why. Then, one day, I was camping at a spot on the border between Victoria and South Australia. That's when everything changed. That's when the Holy Spirit started drawing me in.' Angelina paused. 'I was drawing a picture, by the water. Back then, I was always writing or drawing or painting something. That day, two people came up to me. They said, "What are you doing?" I told them my story. I said I was on my way to Perth and my car wasn't going very well. The lady said, "Would you like us to pray for your journey and for your car?" I said yes, that would be nice. Then they did. She and her husband and I held hands. They were Christians.

'I'd never known anything outside of the Catholic religion before. They prayed for my needs and they spoke about Jesus. Then the lady started praying in tongues. I'd never heard it before, but it sounded nice. I knew about Pentecost, so I knew what it was. I immediately wanted to pray in tongues like that. I was fascinated by this new and beautiful language, and I wanted to ask them about it. I wanted to know more, but they had to leave quickly.'

Angelina explained to me that up until that time, she felt she'd been subject to a spirit of fascination – especially to every occult thing – and now, without realising it, she was about to meet a totally different spirit – the Spirit of God. Angelina then drove to Adelaide and couldn't stop thinking about the two people praying in tongues. She wanted to know more. She arrived in Adelaide and, for some reason, the doors were closed again, even the doors of the Peace Pilgrim follower, so she ended up staying with a contact from her childhood – a Catholic friend.

One night, Angelina and her friend were watching television, and they happened to see an interview with an American Catholic nun. She was being questioned on Australian national television and she was asked, 'Do you speak in tongues?' The nun said, 'Yes, I do.' Angelina couldn't believe it.

Angelina decided she had to find out more about tongues. The next day, she went straight to the Catholic bookshop and she asked the assistant if they had a book on the Holy Spirit, or on tongues. The lady said, 'No, sorry, we don't.' Then Angelina went to another book store. She asked the same thing. The man said 'No, sorry, we don't.' But he did know a church where Angelina could find out more.

'I think he sensed my curiosity,' smiled Angelina. 'It was my curiosity that nearly killed me earlier in my life, and now it was leading me in the right direction. I got back in my car and I found the church that he said to go to. Underneath the church there was a wonderful bookshop. So I walked up to the desk . . . and I asked the same thing. The lady at the desk made a phone call. Then she turned to me and said, "The pastor can see you now." I thought, I only want a book . . . and what's a pastor, anyway? But I was still curious. So I decided, "What can I lose?" I went upstairs and I met the pastor. We both sat down and I told him about my trip to Perth and my New Age stuff. I was proud of it. He listened. He didn't raise an eyebrow. Then he took something out of his pocket. It was a Bible. He started reading it to me. He said, "Do you believe you are a sinner?"'

Angelina paused in the story. 'I hadn't thought about sin for a long time,' she said, 'so I told the man that. Then I said, "Yes, I guess I am." He said, "Do you believe that Jesus died for your sins?" I paused . . . and he kept talking. After a while, I conceded. I just knew. I was a sinner and I needed saving. Somehow, I got the revelation straight away. Jesus died for me and all my sins were forgiven. I wouldn't need to go to confession ever again. I prayed the "sinner's prayer" with him. Then he prayed for me that I would receive the Holy Spirit.

'At first as he prayed, it felt like I was being strangled. I couldn't speak. I wondered what was going on. Then the pastor went out of the room, and he came back with a young lady, and they both prayed for me and I was released. I started immediately singing in tongues. It was like in Acts 10, when the apostle Peter arrived at the house of Cornelius. That's exactly how it happened to me. I started to speak in tongues. It was amazing.

'Afterwards, I went outside and the grass was greener and the sky was blue. I knew the gospel was true. It was 2 May 1988. I was

57 years old and I realised that Jesus died for me. I trusted him and I became God's child in that moment, born again, adopted, forgiven and accepted. It was seventeen years after I had prayed Psalm 104. I even noticed a habitual sin that I'd had since I was a child, just went away . . . and a new psalm became my life's scripture. It was Psalm 18:19. "He delivered me because He delighted in me"' (NKJV).

At this point in the story, I stared at Angelina. She smiled back at me. 'It's an amazing story, isn't it?'

I agreed with her, thinking that God *is* amazing, especially the way he deals with us so individually and uniquely . . . and that I'd never heard of anyone who had come to faith through hearing someone else speaking in tongues. However, in Angelina's story, it fitted. I wondered what happened next.

Angelina said that the pastor and the young lady invited her to join a class for new Christians. She signed up for it straight away because she wanted to find out more about Jesus. Then she went back and told her Catholic friend what had happened. She wanted to tell everyone. Angelina visited a few churches in Adelaide and she attended the course and she began to read the Gospel of John, starting from verse 1. '"In the beginning was the Word,"' said Angelina, '"and the Word was with God, and the Word was God." Amazing!' she smiled. 'I kept reading it. I felt like truth was being inserted in my mind, little by little. I was amazed by the love of God. It seemed incredible that an almighty God who had a trillion things to attend to, stars and planets to keep on their courses, and billions of souls to care about . . . that he would pay attention to one sorry, sinful soul like me . . . one without any talent of any kind, and without any hope for a decent future, and without anything to offer the God of all creation. Why would he do that? What kind of love is this?'

Back at her friend's house, Angelina decided that she needed to get rid of all of her New Age books. There was an open fire in the house, so that was handy, and all the books went in. Then she wondered what to do with her crystals. She took them all down to the Adelaide pier one night and threw them into the water. It was her response to the love of God.

'That was the start of something big,' said Angelina. 'I never did get as far as Perth. But I began to pray the Word. I prayed the Lord's Prayer over a lady and her pain went away. The Lord kept showing me new things. He began to clean me out, but it took a long time. It didn't happen all at once. I would go along merrily with the Lord, and then one day he'd say, "What about that?" and I would deal with the new thing. One day I apologised to all of my children. I sent them each a letter asking for their forgiveness.

'Quite soon after I was born again, I started to ask the Lord if he would use me. I couldn't wait to be put into service. I said, "I've waited too long, Lord! Please . . . let's get on with it." I was 57! It was time.'

Later that year, Angelina said that God gave her a burden and a love for the Jewish people. She began to pray for them. Then she heard about a small Judeo-Islamic sect that began in the 1600s but was still in existence, in the country of Turkey. At the time, Angelina was attending a course at the YWAM base in Canberra, and she felt compelled to go to Turkey and to pray for the people from that sect.

In 1991, when Angelina was 60, she left Australia and went on a twelve-month trip to Israel to do further training at the YWAM School of Missions. During that time she was also able to visit Turkey for two months, and she travelled around Istanbul as well as down the coast to Izmir, meeting people and praying. One of the people she met then was from the Judeo-Islamic sect, for whom she had been praying for some time. 'All I wanted to do was to pray,' said Angelina, 'I wanted to meet with people who I could pray with, and pray for. I wanted to become part of a prayer movement.' After a while, Angelina also went east to Ankara, where she met the leader of YWAM. The leader asked her if she would like to come and stay and serve with them in Turkey. Angelina said yes, she would like to, but first she would need to go back to Australia and pack up her belongings. So shortly afterwards she returned to Australia, and packed, said goodbye to her friends and family, and then three months later moved permanently to Turkey.

'Just like that?' I said.

'Yes,' said Angelina. 'I stayed in Turkey for twenty-three years. For fourteen of those years, I was based in a city called Gaziantep, which is 97 kilometres north of Aleppo, on the border with Syria.'

Later, I found Gaziantep on the map. It made me wonder what Angelina's children thought about their mother moving to the border of Turkey and Syria, in her sixties.

'Some of them weren't that happy about it,' admitted Angelina, 'and I missed them. By the time I was living in Turkey, I had five children, eighteen grandchildren, seven great-grandchildren, and their spouses and partners. But we would write to each other, and later there was phone and the Internet and Skype. I stayed on in Turkey, even through the hard times.'

One of the hard times occurred in May 2009, said Angelina. That day, she went out as usual to the shops near her apartment in Gaziantep. It was a beautiful spring morning, and she went to the bank and the supermarket and the post office. She prayed as she went, as she always did, so thankful for the Lord's love and peace. Afterwards, she got on a bus and came home. But she didn't realise that a man was following her. He hid behind a partition as she unlocked the door to her apartment on the fifth floor. Then he came in behind her. He grabbed her and dragged her to another room, his hand firmly over her mouth. Angelina couldn't breathe or call out. 'I tried to call out to Jesus,' she said, 'but I couldn't.

'His hands were over my mouth. He was trying to strangle me. I'd never been roughed up before. Then he pulled my bag from over my head. That's when I went limp. It was like the Holy Spirit put me in "dead dog" pose. I just lay there on the floor, not shaking or moving, but waiting for the next thing.'

Angelina went very still and quiet. 'Then I heard the front door close,' she said. 'The man had gone. I think he thought he'd killed me. By then it was 1 o'clock in the afternoon, and I lay on the floor, frothing at the mouth, still struggling to breathe. But the first thing that crossed my mind was thankfulness. I was so happy to be alive! I couldn't thank Jesus enough.'

Angelina explained that she then managed to get off the floor and walk into her bedroom where she had a landline. She called two of her friends and they came straight away. Then the police arrived and they took fingerprints. After that, Angelina went to the hospital and, later, the man was found and charged in the high court of Turkey.

'It was hard and it took time,' said Angelina, 'but gradually the Lord healed me of my fear. My neck still ached but I found I could go outside again. I could enjoy the world. I could pray and work. I found out later that at the time of the assault, my intercessory prayer friends were praying for me in Israel. They had a vision of Turkey as a baby in the womb about to be strangled by the cord. So they prayed for me specifically that day! And I give thanks to God for them. Later I remember reading Jesus' words in John 15:19. He said, "you do not belong to the world," and that felt true. I was 78 years old, a pilgrim on the earth, living in Turkey, but inextricably part of God's kingdom . . . so I wrote home to my family and I said that I still felt glad to be here.' Angelina smiled. 'It's a great privilege to join God on his adventures.'

At this point in talking to Angelina, it was obvious to me that she meant the things she said, deeply. It wasn't one of those superficial, victorious pronouncements that some people might employ. Angelina sat quietly beside me and I sensed her joy in the Lord. But then she told me that the assault was the first of three incidents. Ten months later, spring arrived again in Turkey and Angelina went to see the tulips in a town nearby, with a friend. Afterwards, she caught the minibus home. There was a crowd on it that day. A large woman tried to change seats while the bus was moving and, at that moment, the bus jerked and the large woman fell straight on top of Angelina – onto her chest and front – the areas that had only recently healed from their previous injury and bruising. Angelina went back to see the doctor and she was put on medication for neurological pain. It spread all over her body and she couldn't walk very well for a while. But she recovered over time.

'I kept reading Psalm 18,' said Angelina. 'It says the Lord defends us. He doesn't bring the trouble, he's with us. And that's true. I called to the Lord and he heard me . . . and my heart still sang. Psalm 18 also says, 'You exalted me above my foes; from a violent man you rescued me. Therefore I will praise you, LORD, among the nations; I will sing the praises of your name.'

Angelina kept praising God and serving him. She explained that some years earlier she had bought her own apartment in Gaziantep. 'The Lord led me to it,' she said. 'It was a lighthouse, a place of prayer and worship and refuge . . . We would meet to pray, sometimes multiple times a week. That was our work.'

Then, in July 2015, Angelina was out walking and she fell on an uneven path, injuring her shoulder. 'It was so bruised,' she said. 'I went to the hospital again. It was not long afterwards that I returned to Australia.'

I asked Angelina if it was hard to return, or if she had thought about returning earlier.

'No,' she said. 'I never thought about leaving my post. I knew the Lord had put me there for a purpose, and I always had a thing about not leaving my post until I was properly relieved of it.'

Apparently, though, not long after Angelina injured her shoulder, a new couple arrived to work in Gaziantep, and they were able to relieve her of her post. The two of them now live in her apartment and they are carrying on the ministry of prayer and worship.

'Perhaps it was the Lord's way of getting me out of there,' admitted Angelina. 'It was getting very difficult in that area of Turkey. ISIS were already there by then.'

We both paused, wondering about God's timing. 'What do you think now, about the way God has worked in your life?' I asked.

'When I look back now,' said Angelina, 'I see that God is like a fisherman. The Holy Spirit put his bait on a hook. It began when I was a child, taking communion, and then when I made a promise at 11. He honoured that promise. Even at 40, when I prayed and called out to the Lord, he heard me. He was there. The Holy Spirit is tenacious. He gave me the prayer and he kept me going for another seventeen years. And then without exercising any urgency, or being at all pushy, he waited until the Father said, "Now", and then he silently and gently dropped his line into the muddy waters of my life. He landed me. He took me out of the sea of filth and he deposited me in the river of life, never to return to that old way of life again. I was home safe, with the one who loved me the most.'

I smiled at the analogy and agreed with her. I wondered, 'Do you ever think about why God waited another seventeen years, after that time when you were 40? Could he have revealed himself to you earlier?'

'He could have,' smiled Angelina, 'but I don't think it would have worked . . . because *I* wasn't ready. I was still curious about so many things. I had to get to the point of disappointment with everything . . . and then I was ready for the Holy Spirit. I just knew it was true. I was a new creation. I realised that God's heart of love is so big. It's bigger than a million oceans and a trillion stars and planets. He's always close. He was close . . . when my husband left. It says in Psalm 34 that when we are most distressed, he steps in. "The LORD is close to the broken-hearted and saves those who are crushed in spirit." And that's so true.

'I haven't always made right choices. I haven't been good. Yet somehow the insistent, persistent love of God has stepped in. Time after time, he has redirected me for his purposes. And it doesn't matter how old we are, the Holy Spirit is still at work in us. Even now, I'm 86, and I still take communion every day,' Angelina smiled. 'It's still the most important thing. I want to "proclaim the Lord's death until he comes".[3] The blood of Jesus has made me whole, and he has made me worthy to be his child.'

By this point in the story, of course, I'd finished my lemon and ginger tea with honey, so I got up and began to say goodbye to Angelina, and to thank her. As I did, she handed me a parable that she had written while she was in Turkey. It was a story about a small stone that was found on the ground, by a king. The stone began its life looking dirty and worthless, but the king took the stone home and he asked his experts to work on it. The experts worked over time, and the stone was cleaned and heated and brushed and cut. The process hurt the stone quite a lot and it made a fuss. But every time the stone fussed, the king sang to it and comforted it. Occasionally, the king even gave the stone a little rest. The process went on . . . until the little stone emerged as a ruby, sparkling and brilliant.

Angelina smiled. 'We are all like that ruby. We have to go through change. Sometimes it hurts a lot and we make a fuss. But in the story, the king cared for the stone, he comforted it, he sang to it and he gave it a rest. God is like that. He's making us all into precious gemstones. He is never in a hurry with us, but he's always on time – making something beautiful, through his Holy Spirit – as we yield to him and point to him, in everything. That's why, in everything, it's *his* story, not mine.'

I agreed with her, and thanked her again and left, thinking about the precious, 86-year-old gemstone, whose mind was still curious, and whose story was God's.

11

Clean on the inside

Jamshed and Matluba – former Soviet Union

Jamshed and Matluba currently live on a bare hillside on the outskirts of a major city in the Ferghana Valley, in the former Soviet Union. I first heard about their story through a mutual friend, Kara. Kara and her husband, Shaun, and their four children also lived in that same valley for five years. They shared life with Jamshed and Matluba and developed a rich friendship with them, amidst bitter winters and baking hot summers and colourful celebrations over food and dancing, all in the shadow of the Turkestan mountain range. After returning to Australia, Kara told me that she really missed her friends. She often thought of them on their hillside. Then she happened to mention that Jamshed and Matluba had previously practised a version of folk-Islam, and that they had come to faith in Jesus through a series of dreams. I wanted to find out more, so I asked Kara if we could Skype her friends in the Ferghana Valley.

'Sure,' said Kara. So, a few months later, I drove to their house and the three of us gathered in their living room. We put the call through to the Ferghana Valley. While we waited for Jamshed and Matluba to answer the call, my friends explained to me that Jamshed's English was really good. 'We all worked for the same NGO during those years,' said Kara. 'Jamshed was employed as our translator, which is why his English is good. He also helped with the community health work in the villages, and we all spent a lot of time together. But Matluba only speaks the local languages. She doesn't speak any English.'

Then the call went through. 'They're online,' said my friends excitedly, as both Jamshed and Matluba appeared on the screen, smiling and laughing and sending greetings to us all in the local language. My friends introduced me, and I also smiled and thanked them for being online, all the while feeling rather wonderful that we could sit here in Sydney and chat with them in the Ferghana Valley.

I began by asking Jamshed about his childhood and his background in folk-Islam. Jamshed explained to me that he came from a village in the north of the country and that his mother was a *fulbin*. That meant that she was a spiritist. *Fulbins* exert special spiritual power through rituals, so the people in the town used to come to Jamshed's house every day, seeking healing from his mother if they were ill, or if they had other forms of need, and she would perform rituals over them.

'They would come all the time,' said Jamshed. 'I remember my mother would hang thistles on the door, and she would put chillis around the house, and perform rituals over the people. They even came at night, and they would come back regularly, so it must have been working.'

'Did your family believe in one God, over all?' I asked.

'Yes,' said Jamshed. 'In our thinking there is one big, powerful God. But he is very distant and a long way away. We think that when a baby is 4 months old in the womb, God writes their destiny on their forehead. He is very powerful . . . but he's not personable or knowable and there's a big gap between us and him, so we need something to fill it – something here and now that will protect us – something tangible. That's why my mother hangs thistles on the door, and sprinkles chicken blood . . . and puts chillis around the house, and wears her amulets. She thinks they protect her, or they gain God's favour. That's why everyone in the town comes to her house for the rituals, all of the time, so they can also gain favour and be protected.'

'What did you think of the rituals yourself, as you were growing up?' I asked.

'I used to believe in them,' said Jamshed. 'I was young and I saw people visiting my mother and I observed that they kept coming back to do the rituals. So I thought the rituals must be working. That's why they came back regularly. My mother's brother was also a *duomullah* – that's a respected prayer leader within the Islamic faith. He would go and visit people in their homes and pray for them. He used to say to us that if you trust in it – in the rituals and spells – then it will happen, that thing that you want. It will work. I thought the people must be trusting in the spells and I saw that it was working,' Jamshed paused. 'But then, over time, it didn't always work. For example, I remember one boy who came to see my mother. He said he loved a girl and he wanted to marry her. But the girl didn't show any interest in him. So my mother gave the boy some chocolate and she put the spell in the chocolate. She said to the boy, "Give the girl this chocolate and she will eat it and she will be interested in you." The boy did what my mother said but, over time, I saw that the girl was not interested in him. They did not get married. It didn't happen . . .'

When Jamshed finished his schooling, he worked for a while as a part-time English teacher, and then he was offered work translating for the NGO. It was a great opportunity, and Jamshed said he really enjoyed it, but the work was still part-time and he wished that he could have more of it. He would often talk to his uncle, the *duomullah*, about his work situation. 'My uncle would say that I need to do the rituals,' said Jamshed. 'He would say, "You are dirty on the inside. That's why you are not getting more work." Then my uncle would tell me to come to him and do the rituals and, if I did them, I would be clean on the inside.

'I remember one day, my uncle told me I must drink 2 litres of milk. He said that if I did, I would vomit after I drank it, but I would be clean on the inside and my work would be better. So I drank all that milk and I vomited, but I remember that nothing changed with my work situation. So then I thought that it was because I was confused. Perhaps I didn't trust it enough. If I trusted it, if I believed it enough, then it would happen. It's not a physical thing, you can't see it, it's on the inside. But I tried it and nothing happened. My work situation didn't improve. I still felt dirty on the inside. I think I always felt dirty on the inside and I wanted to know how I could get clean.'

Listening to Jamshed, I thought it was interesting that he described himself as feeling dirty on the inside. So I mentioned that, in the West, we don't often use that description about ourselves. Kara and Shaun agreed with me. 'Yes,' they said. 'But being clean is a really big thing in the Ferghana Valley. People are always washing themselves, all the time – they wash their hands and their feet before they do anything in the house and, of course, before they pray *salat* – that's the ritual five-times-a-day prayers. Generally, it's very important culturally to be clean and to have a clean home . . . so they spend hours each day sweeping their yard and street to get rid of the dust. It's connected to honour. If the person is not clean, then there is no honour. The people feel shamed if they're dirty on the outside. It's the same on the inside.'

Jamshed agreed with them. 'I wanted to know how I could get clean on the inside,' he said. 'That was my question. So one day I started to talk to another fellow-worker in our organisation. He was a Christian and his name was Adam. He was learning the local language and, as part of that, we were reading his book, *First Steps*.[1] The book went through the Bible, mostly the *Injil*, and it talked about what it meant to follow Jesus and become more like him. I thought the book was interesting, and I wanted to know more. Parts of it seemed to suggest that the rituals and spells my mother practised were not that helpful. It said that the things a *fulbin* does can be evil . . . so that's when I started to question those things and not believe in them.'

Not long after that, in 2010, Jamshed said that he was driving to a small predominantly Russian town with his uncle, the *duomullah*. The town was on the outskirts of the city and they were on their way to a Russian Orthodox church, because the *duomullah* wanted to pick up some candles – special large candles for his rituals.

'If a *duomullah* lights a special candle,' said Jamshed, 'and prays special things for a person, then the smoke will go to the person and they will be fine. That's what they believe. So, the *duomullah* and I went into the town to a special Russian Orthodox church because they had special candles there. At the time I had never been to any kind of church before. I remember it was evening and the road was bumpy. When we got to the church I got out of the car, and I saw that there were pictures on the windows. I walked in to the church, and I saw one of the pictures inside was of Mary holding her son Jesus in her arms. At once, as I looked at it, something like joy came into my heart. I was happy. I felt relief when I looked at the picture. I had heard about Jesus through my friend Adam, and reading the book, so I knew who it was. Then, when I came out of the church, I started to think about the picture . . . It made me want to know more about Jesus. Who was he? So the next week in the language class, I asked Adam more questions about Jesus. I found out more about him. It was like God started to open my heart.'

'Wow!' I smiled. 'That's great.'

'Yes,' said Jamshed. 'The *duomullah* found his special candles, but I found something better. I kept asking Adam questions about Jesus. I was also a bit confused. I wanted to know, "Is it true or not, what Adam is saying?" Then, after a time, while I was still questioning, I had a dream.

'In my dream, Adam was coming out of his house towards me, and his clothes were shining and white. His family were there with him too, and they all had shining white clothes on, like Adam. Suddenly in my heart I knew that what Adam was saying to me about Jesus and the Bible was true, because he was a clean person. He had found out how to be clean. When I woke up from the dream, I knew that I should listen to the things that Adam was saying, because he was clean, and I could find out how to get clean clothes, also.'

After that, Jamshed kept talking with Adam. He told Adam about the dream that he'd had, and Adam was very encouraged by it. 'But I still had questions,' said Jamshed. 'I was still . . . confused. Is Jesus the Son of God, and God as well? I remember that I told Adam one day that I was still a bit confused. "If only God could come to me in a dream and explain it all to me, then I would believe in Jesus!" Then I kept having dreams!

'In one of the dreams, I was outside on the street with my neighbours and my friends, and I could see different kinds of animals coming towards us – horses and bears and camels. So I said something to my friends about the animals, but when I said that about the animals, my friends in the dream said they couldn't see the animals. It was only me that could see the animals. When I woke up from the dream, I was still thinking about it. Why could I see the animals and they couldn't? Later, I told the dream to Adam and he told me that what I was now seeing, in the truths of the Bible, other people couldn't see. He said it says in the Bible that not everybody can see and understand.

'The dream gave me a real sense of encouragement that what I was seeing and believing, in Jesus, was true. I could come to Christ. It was difficult, but God opened my eyes that day so that I could see. I think that if God had not opened my eyes, I would not have understood. So I kept reading the Bible with Adam – especially the *Injil*.'

'Was there something in particular that stood out to you, the first time you read the *Injil*?' I asked.

'Yes,' said Jamshed. 'Jesus said to Peter, "Who do you think I am?" Peter replied, "You are the Son of God, the Messiah." When I read that, I started to think that until God opens our eyes, we cannot see that Jesus is the Son of God. Jesus said to Peter that the Father in heaven had revealed it to him. He had already asked his disciples, "Who do the crowds say I am?" And the disciples replied, "Some say John the Baptist; others say Elijah; and still others that one of the prophets of long ago has come back to life."[2]

'Not everyone will see and understand who Jesus is. It was a real encouragement to me. It helped me to pray a lot, to open my heart to God. I knew that God would explain things to me, and one day I would understand fully. So I prayed a lot and I read the Bible. I said to God, "I don't want to follow the rituals anymore. I want you to clean me from the inside." God did that. One day I had a dream. I was pulling a black hair out of myself. It was a dirty hair. I had difficulty pulling it out. Then it all came out, in one go! I realised then that God did it. God made me clean through his Son, Jesus. He did it! I didn't need to see the *duomullah* anymore. I knew that I was clean. Jesus took all my sin when he died on the cross, and now he wants to change me on the inside.'

By then, in late 2010, Jamshed was 27. He and Matluba had been married for three years. Jamshed explained that Matluba grew up in a nearby village, but her family didn't practise religion in the same way that his family did. For the first few years of their marriage, both Jamshed and Matluba lived with Jamshed's family – in one small room of the family house. It was very difficult. Their first two daughters arrived in quick succession and then the room seemed even smaller. It contained one bed, two small mattresses in the corner, and a coal heater in the other corner. As well as that, it was not the norm, culturally, for Jamshed and Matluba to be living with Jamshed's family. In the Ferghana Valley, it is only the youngest son who should stay at home with the family, while all the others should move out. But Jamshed could not afford to move.

At this point in our Skype call, I was imagining Matluba with her two small daughters (and one on the way), living with her in-laws, one of whom was a *fulbin,* and I really wanted to hear her story! So Matluba came online and she smiled and explained, in the local language, that her life had been quite difficult. Her father was an alcoholic and her mother was absent for many years, working in Russia, so Matluba grew up living with her grandmother.

'I don't remember thinking about God as a child,' said Matluba. 'My family were not religious. They didn't believe in anything. I had never heard the name of Jesus, so I never thought about anything. But we had a television. One day when I was about 14, I remember I saw a film about Noah. I thought it was interesting. I watched that film all the way through and I never forgot about it. I kept thinking about it. It had a place in my heart. Then, when Jamshed began thinking about Jesus, at first he didn't talk to me much about it. He didn't explain it to me. But he took me to visit with Adam's wife, June. When we went to their house, I felt different. I felt relief. I felt peace when I was there. So I wanted to know where the peace came from.

'I asked Jamshed, "What kind of book are you reading with Adam?" He told me about *First Steps.* Before that, I had never heard about Jesus. I had never even heard the name. I had heard about other prophets, but never about Jesus. Then when Jamshed told me about Jesus, I felt peace. That's why I started reading the *Injil* on my own.

'At first when I read it, I couldn't understand it, it was in difficult language, but I somehow knew it was important. So on the nights when I couldn't sleep, I put the *Injil* under my pillow . . . and then on those nights, I remember that my heart had peace and I felt happy. I felt strong on those nights.

'But I didn't understand the words at first,' continued Matluba. 'I didn't understand for a long time – until I read more, and then I understood more. I saw after a while that what the *Injil* offered was healing for your problems – whatever your problem was. If you were crying, it had the answer, and if you were sick or in need, it had the answer. For me, I had many problems. And the *Injil* had the answer.'

Matluba explained that, back then, living with Jamshed's family was difficult. There was misunderstanding and trouble. Often, Jamshed's mother would put pressure on Matluba to perform rituals and spells in order to produce a son, after having (by then) three daughters. In the Ferghana Valley, it is desolation not to produce a son, so Jamshed's mother told Matluba that she must perform ritual sprinkling and other types of magic to procure a son. But Matluba didn't want to perform the rituals. One day, she told her mother-in-law that she trusted in Jesus for whatever gift he gave them.

'I felt a lot of pressure,' said Matluba, 'until one day, I was reading the Bible and I realised that God was with me, all of the time. Jesus said he will be with us always[3] . . . even in this house, with the *fulbin*. I was so moved, I just had to dance. Of course, there was not much room to dance in our small room, so I got up . . . and I danced on the bed. I felt such a joy in the Lord. Then our daughters came in and saw me, and they wanted to know what I was doing – why I was dancing. I told them about my joy in the Lord because God was with me . . . and then they joined in too. We were all dancing on the bed!'

We all laughed at the image of Matluba and her daughters dancing on her bed, out of joy in the Lord.

'Were there Christian churches in that area in those days?' I asked.

Kara and Shaun explained that, yes, there were some Christian churches in those years; however the services were mostly in Russian, and dominated by Russian forms, rather than local forms . . . and Matluba, as well as many of the other locals couldn't understand enough Russian to engage well with the service. It had, by then, been nineteen years since the Soviet Union dissolved into twelve independent republics. In their area there was definitely a need for house churches that could be run in the local language, for and by local believers, reaching out to others in an organic way. But in 2010, in that area of the Ferghana Valley, there were very few Christians.

At the same time as that, though, Kara and Matluba were becoming close friends. On arriving in the country, Kara had struggled to home-school their three older children at the same time as care for their youngest daughter, who was only 2 . . . so she offered paid work to Matluba. Could Matluba work in their home, caring for their 2-year-old, while Kara home-schooled the other three? The solution worked well and it meant that Kara and Matluba regularly had the opportunity to read the Bible together and talk about their struggles and their faith. It turned into a beautifully rich fellowship.

However, daily life didn't immediately improve for Jamshed and Matluba. By then, Matluba's brother was in jail, her father was still an alcoholic and her mother was still working in Russia. And there they were, living with Jamshed's family, when they shouldn't have been.

'One day, during all of that, Kara made me a cake,' said Matluba, smiling. 'Nobody had ever made me a cake before. It made me feel special. She showed me love and I felt that God was doing something in my life. He was making me stronger.

'Some years after that, my brother died, in jail. My family came together and they wailed. They all prayed for his soul for a set amount of days. I grieved with them and I tried to wail with them. I wanted to wail. It is a great shame if you don't wail at a funeral of someone you love . . . but when I tried to wail, I found that no sound came out of my mouth. I stood there and grieved with them, but I couldn't wail, and I didn't want to join them in the prayers for his soul. They noticed that I didn't pray for his soul and they asked me why. I said that I couldn't pray for his soul because it was between him and God. Jesus had already done all that was needed to save us. They were OK with that, but they still put pressure on us to join in the rituals.'

In 2014 Jamshed and Matluba decided it was time to leave Jamshed's family home. The government were giving out free blocks of land on a nearby rocky hillside. It was the least desirable place to live in the area. The hill was a pile of rubble, near the tip, with no trees and no roads and no other houses on the hill. It was completely bare. But Jamshed and Matluba said yes to the offer of a block of land. When Jamshed and Matluba told Kara and Shaun that they had decided to move to the rocky hillside, Kara and Shaun were a bit shocked. The hillside was baking hot in the summer and bitterly cold in winter, and windy all the time. The winds would pick up the rubbish and blow it all across the hill until it collected in the ditches. And at night the wild dogs would come. Kara and Shaun questioned the wisdom of moving there.

Jamshed and Matluba started building a small two-roomed house on the hill out of cement blocks, with a toilet in the middle. There was no power or water available. Kara and Shaun went to visit them regularly while they were building, and they continued to worry. Their friends were moving into a house on a hillside, out of town, with no transport, and Matluba didn't drive. Wouldn't she be isolated?

Now, both Jamshed and Matluba say, 'Actually, God put us on the hillside.' Matluba explained to us in the local language, 'After we built on the hillside, other people slowly started to build as well. Then they would come and ask us for help with their electricity, which was connected later. Or they wanted us to give their children a bath. Or sometimes I gave them a meal. I love to bake meals and cheesecakes . . . I hang out my washing and I sing praise songs, and the people hear me and they ask me about the songs.'

One day, Matluba said, she decided to give an *Injil* to a needy local woman on the hillside. She knew that, in their country, she should be careful about sharing her faith publicly but, as a local Christian, she was allowed to own Christian literature herself, and read it, and possibly share it with her friends. So that day Matluba gave her neighbour an *Injil*. The next day the woman came back and knocked on Matluba's door.

'I've read the book,' she said in the local language, 'and I like it! I think we should meet regularly to read it and pray together.'

Matluba was surprised at first, but then she began to meet regularly with her neighbour, and she asked Kara for advice about where to start in their Bible reading. Over time, word spread on the hillside and a few of the other women also asked if they could borrow the book – even quite a devout Muslim neighbour!

Matluba smiled, relaying the story to us. She said that at first when she gave out the *Injil* she had felt very nervous. 'I've always been a timid person,' she said. 'But somehow God helped me to do it and I feel different now. I want to share what I believe. And my neighbours are interested! Maybe that's why God put us on the hillside.'

Kara and Shaun smiled too. 'At first we were praying for house churches in the local language and for local believers,' they said, 'and nothing was really happening. Then Jamshed and Matluba decided to move to the hillside and we didn't think they should. It was too isolated. But now there they are on the hillside, and some of the women are meeting and they're sharing Jesus and the people are actually interested and they're reading the Bible together, in the local language.' They paused. 'We still think it's a really difficult place to live . . . but Matluba doesn't complain. She has a joyful heart, she still sings and dances. She has four daughters now! And she's always singing praise songs at home . . . She even sings when the neighbours are visiting . . .'

At this point in the story we all paused and looked at some of Kara and Shaun's photos – with all four of them in Jamshed and Matluba's small concrete block house on the hillside, eating food together on a tablecloth laid out on the floor, and all the children outside, dressed in colourful clothes. There were views over the town, which looked dry and arid at first glance, but there were glimpses of the Turkestan mountain range in the distance.

Kara explained that she had taught Matluba how to make cheesecakes, and in the Ferghana Valley, of course, it's important that food, like most clothing, is glittery and beautiful! So Kara and Matluba made glittery cakes together. Three years later Matluba is baking them herself, in her little house on the bare hillside, and selling them at the local restaurants, as well as taking special orders. People are paying good local prices – nearly $3 for one wedge. Kara is amazed.

'What do your family think now,' I asked Jamshed, 'about your faith in Jesus?'

Jamshed smiled. 'My mother is still practising as a *fulbin*. But not so long ago I was talking to my father, and he said to me, "Jamshed, I'm a Muslim, but if what happened to you happened to me as well then, of course, I would become a Christian too." So I pray for that to happen for my father; I pray for my whole family, that they will be saved. We praise God that we don't have a bad relationship with any of them now because of our belief. But we are praying that God will open their minds and hearts.

'I know that I'm different to what I was. I'm clean now. Whenever I have problems, I pray to God. Everything is different. I haven't been back to the *duomullah*. I still have problems, and I still get stressed about work – about providing for my growing family – but I know that God is in control and I can bring it to God. So that makes my whole life different. I don't need to do those other ritual things I used to do. I can go straight to God. If I have problems, I know what to do. Everything has changed.'

Matluba came back online and explained that she and Jamshed were baptised in the river, in September 2014, just after they moved into their house on the hillside. Recently, one of her friends has been asking for baptism.

'I tried to explain everything to her about Jesus,' said Matluba. 'I told her that difficulties might come if she followed Jesus. But she has to make her own choice. She has decided that she wants to be baptised, and now I meet with her every fortnight to learn and share more about following Jesus. All of the time, I pray. That's what's changed for me. When I first said the Lord's Prayer, my faith became stronger. I realised then that prayer was powerful. I prayed from my heart that first time, and my faith came. So I keep praying. I pray for all my family – that they will know the Lord, like we do.'

We all smiled and said "thank you". As we finished the Skype call, we assured Jamshed and Matluba that we would keep praying for them all, on their rocky hillside in the Ferghana Valley, and we would pray for their four daughters, and for their wider families, and for all their neighbours on the hillside as they meet to read the *Injil* in the local language.

'And maybe,' I said, 'some of the people who read this story will want to pray for you too.'

'Imagine that!' said Jamshed and Matluba, together.

12

More powerful than the Voodoo

Carine and Alberic – Benin

Carine is a gorgeous young African girl. She has eyes that dance and hands that want to share expressively in the story. She is trained as a medical doctor and married to Yannick, with two young daughters. I first met Carine on a beautiful spring morning in Australia, and she explained to me that her background was in Voodoo belief and practice. Of course, I wanted to know more, so I kept asking her questions, and she kept answering them in her excited, hurried way, hardly pausing for breath. She began by saying that she grew up in Benin, a tiny, French-speaking nation in West Africa. Benin, with its population of 10 million people, has a seaport at the Gulf of Guinea, and it is the birthplace of the Voodoo religion.

'When you Google our nation,' said Carine, 'the first thing you see is Voodoo. It's the traditional religion. It's our culture. It's even bigger than the culture, it's our belief system. It's the oldest thing. It rules everything. The first thing we know is Voodoo.

'When I was growing up in the 1980s, almost everyone was a Voodoo-Animist. Every family or village had their own Voodoo spirit. They would say, "This mountain is my Voodoo" or "This river is my Voodoo", or sometimes their Voodoo would be the ground or a metal or a rainbow or a mermaid. In my mum's ethnic group, the Voodoo was the python, so they would never kill pythons in her village. Sometimes a village has lots and lots of Voodoo spirits.'

'Do people also believe in one God overall?' I asked.

'There is one God, called Mahu,' said Carine. 'Mahu is in charge of everything, he rules everything, and he decides everything. But he is very distant. No one can speak to him, so there are many Voodoo spirits, maybe two hundred of them, little gods, to talk to. Some people say there are good parts and bad parts to Voodoo. The good part is that there is a system of punishment. If someone does something wrong – if they don't follow the Voodoo rules, of which there are many – then they are taken by the Voodoo priest to the temple; it's a place in the forest, made of logs and sticks. Only the priest can enter. The person is punished. Everyone else is forbidden to go there. One of my uncles was a Voodoo priest, so he had a pact with the Voodoos for life. They owned his body and his life . . . and when he died, the other priests took his body to the forest. We don't know what they did with it. Maybe they buried it, or maybe they used his parts for rituals and spells.'

'Were you fearful of the Voodoos as you were growing up?' I asked.

'Always,' said Carine. 'The Voodoo spirits come out at night to check on the town. They make a sound like a whirling through the air. It's so loud, it's like someone is hurling a rope.' Carine paused and whipped her right arm around in circles, making a whooshing sound, like the wind. 'Like this,' she said. 'You can hear it from 10 kilometres away. It sounds like the wind, but we know what it is.

'I was so scared of the Voodoo. I'd stay awake all night if I heard it. Sometimes the Voodoo would come to our front door and just stay there. No one can go outside when it comes out, so we could never see it. If we went out, we would be killed. Only the Voodoo priest can go out. I was really scared of the Voodoo. I'd hear it a lot.

'Sometimes the Voodoo calls a person to go and do certain things. My aunt was a Voodoo priest and her Voodoo spirit was the mermaid. It's called the Mami Wata – the Voodoo spirit from the sea. It's very frightening. Sometimes the Mami Wata would call my aunt to come into the sea and she would go . . . and not come back for hours or days. She just disappeared – became invisible. We never knew what happened.'

Back then, Carine and her family were living in a town called Cotonou – down the south, near the sea. The family included four younger brothers and sisters, and all the children grew up speaking French as well as three local languages.

'We would go and stay with our friends on holidays, or we'd meet them at the park. My mum was in charge of the post office and my dad was the ship's captain. My dad's name was Alberic. Being the ship's captain meant that he was away at sea a lot, but he was always practising Voodoo. He used to pay the priest to build our own Voodoos – out of grass and sticks and soil and blood and body parts, mostly from animals, but sometimes they would use people's skulls and bones as well. The priest would come to our house every month and slaughter a chicken or a goat, and then it would be mixed together, with the soil and grass, and the whole thing would be formed into a mound that looked like a human – that's the Voodoo. The Voodoo would then be placed in the backyard and sometimes people would poke sticks into it.

'There are so many meanings; for example, if you poke the stick into the Voodoo's heart it will protect your heart. Mostly Voodoos are made to protect people, but some people use them to harm another person – they can put a curse on them and kill them. But my dad never used Voodoo to harm another person, he always used Voodoo to protect himself and his family. He needed a lot of protection, because he was very wealthy, so he began to build more and more Voodoos until they were everywhere – in our bathroom and in the lounge and under the bed. They were all there to protect us.

'The priest kept telling my dad to make more. He'd say that someone was trying to kill his children and my dad would have to give the priest more money, and then they'd build another Voodoo to protect us. We believed it 100 per cent. If we didn't make more Voodoos, we would be killed or something bad would happen to us. Most of the time in Africa, if someone dies, we wonder if it was because of a curse. We ask ourselves why – who cursed him, or which witch killed him?

'We'd have to get more power, or more protection. We'd have to make more Voodoos, all the time.'

At this point in the story, we paused so that Carine could show me photos of Voodoos on her phone – Voodoos of all different shapes and sizes. I tried to imagine them in her garden and under her bed.

'My dad grew up in a village,' she explained, 'in a family of ten children. Back then there was a rule that each family had to choose one child to be educated. Of the ten children in my dad's family, he was chosen. So after high school he went to live in Côte d'Ivoire to get his degree in maritime studies and then he went to France for further training. Not long after that he got a job in the Marines; soon he became a lieutenant, and then he became a captain.

'In 1977 he was offered the position of captain of the first fishing boat in the country of Benin. It was a really powerful position and the boat was huge. Forty people could sleep on it. To captain the boat was a very important position in our country. It meant that he had a lot of money. Because of all the power and the money, he needed a lot of protection. People were jealous of him. They could put a curse on him and take his life, or his money, or his family. So he needed to protect us. That's why he made so many Voodoos.

'As well as that, he would rub a powder on our arms, to protect us. Every weekend, he and the Voodoo priest would burn chickens and grind the carbon and make a powder out of it. Then they would take a blade and make tiny cuts in our forearms, lots of them, all down our arms, and they'd rub the powder into the cuts.' Carine paused and showed me the marks on her arms, still evident thirty years later.

'Did it hurt?' I asked.

'Yes,' said Carine, 'but we were children, we didn't have a choice. The blood would come out of our arms and the powder would sting. But Dad said that if he didn't do it, the witch would kill us. He was fearful of our lives. They used the same blade on everybody, so there was a lot of contamination. It was the same time that HIV/AIDS was spreading throughout Africa, so that was a big problem. Nowadays the government tells the priests they have to change the blades. But back then they used the same blade. And my mum would watch while Dad rubbed the powder in, but she refused to do it herself. She didn't think she needed the Voodoos.'

Carine's mum, Marhysa, had grown up in the city and she believed in Mahu, but she never had Voodoos in her house – not like Alberic. She had decided that being good was enough to protect her.

There was a reason for that. When Marhysa was in her early twenties, she finished her university degree, got a good job and married Alberic. Everything was going so well for her that her sister became jealous of her – so jealous that the sister decided to kill Marhysa with the Voodoo. The sister stole Marhysa's shoe and went to the Voodoo priest so that he would put a curse on Marhysa, through the shoe. But the Voodoo priest knew Marhysa quite well and he thought she was a good girl. The priest liked her because she was respectful, so he didn't feel good about putting the curse on her, and he told the sister that he'd done it, even though he hadn't. Then the priest told the sister that the curse didn't work because Marhysa was a good girl. From then on, Marhysa decided that being good was the best way to protect herself from the Voodoo.

'So my dad did all the Voodoo,' said Carine, 'and he loved us. He was funny, and we loved him a lot. He was a good father to us. But at the same time, he also loved his power and money. He enjoyed the good life! He liked women and alcohol. He had mistresses while he was away from home and also while he was at home. Over time he had two more wives and more children. They all practised Voodoo. Sometimes we met the other wives, but we never told my mum. My dad would tell us not to. He would sleep at home and then during the day he would do whatever he wanted.'

We paused, thinking about Carine's mum.

'She struggled,' admitted Carine. 'She could have divorced him, but her friends kept telling her to stay with the children. They said she had to take care of us – her family . . . So she did. She kept working at the post office, and she was provided for, but she was not happy. Then, one day, my dad had been drinking a lot and he came home and they had an argument and he became violent, so my mum decided to leave. She called her family and the next day they all came over. They brought a van and they put all our stuff into it . . . I think my mum had been preparing. She was building another house nearby and she was going to rent it out, but we moved into it, instead. Grandma came to live with us as well – my mum's mum. Grandma didn't let my dad come and visit, ever, and so Mum and Dad didn't see each other for two years. I was 7 years old when we moved out. But I still saw my dad. He used to come and visit us at school and tell us not to tell my mum – usually for an hour or so, twice a week.'

During the next two years, though, Carine explained that things became more difficult for Alberic. In the early part of 1988, the boat was stolen. That grand fishing vessel, the first of its kind in the country of Benin – the one belonging to the government – somehow vanished overnight, and nobody knew how it happened, or where it went. The authorities searched, and conducted a thorough investigation. There was an uproar because the boat could not be found – not even a trace of it . . . and Alberic took the blame. He was responsible for the boat, so he had to explain it. But he couldn't explain it, and he was taken to the courts. After the trial Alberic was let out on bail, but he was forbidden to leave the city. He lost his job, he lost his income, he lost his power and he lost his lifestyle.

'It was very hard for my dad,' said Carine. 'He began to drink more. Then he became more violent with his other wives, his other children and his other mistresses, so they all left him as well. Then he was alone, he had nothing at all. He became more depressed . . . He didn't know what to do. It went on and on. He just stayed in the house, doing nothing . . . and then in 1989 everything changed.'

One day in early 1989, Alberic had a visit from his cousin, Roland. Roland was a Christian. Roland said to Alberic, 'You know, you need God in your life.'

Alberic just laughed. 'What are you talking about?' he said. 'I've studied. I have a degree. I'm smart. Why would I need God in my life?'

Roland repeated himself, 'You need God in your life.'

'I don't care,' said Alberic. 'Even if God does exist, I have Voodoos in my life.'

Then Roland asked Alberic what he was doing on Sunday. 'Nothing,' said Alberic. 'I'm doing nothing. I'm waiting for the boat to be found.'

'Would you like to go to church with me on Sunday?' asked Roland.

Somehow Alberic agreed, because he couldn't think of a reason not to go. He wasn't doing anything else.

The next Sunday, Roland arrived at 7 a.m. to pick up Alberic for church. At that time there was a small percentage of Christians in Benin, and they met regularly. But when Roland arrived at the house, Alberic was not there. He had changed his mind and decided to leave the house to avoid going to church with Roland. Roland left and he came back the next Sunday, but the same thing happened. Alberic had left the house early. So on the third Sunday, Roland did something different. He arrived at the house even earlier than expected, and Alberic was at home.

'You really want me to go to church?' Alberic said. 'But I know more than your pastors. I am educated! And I have Voodoo! Even so, I will go to make you happy.'

Alberic and Roland went to church that day. The first thing Alberic noticed was that the people smiled at him. They welcomed him. Then a visiting preacher began to speak. The speaker read from Ecclesiastes 1:1–12, and he said that everything in life was about vanity. Everything in the world was vanity and meaningless, including work and the generations and knowledge and even the water cycle. 'All streams flow into the sea, yet the sea is never full.' Life, in all its fullness, is completely empty without God.

'It was amazing,' said Alberic to Carine later. 'When the man was preaching, he was describing my life. But I kept thinking, "He doesn't know me! He didn't know I was coming to church! How does he know me?" Then I thought I might get up . . . but I couldn't get out of my seat. It was like something was holding me there. Afterwards, I knew I needed to talk to the man . . . and Roland introduced us and we talked for two hours. By the end, I decided to follow Jesus.'

Two days later, it seems Alberic decided to get rid of all his Voodoos. He rang the school and he asked the headmistress if Carine could have permission to leave the school and spend half a day with him. 'It's an important day for me,' he explained in the car to Carine. 'I've become a Christian. I want to get rid of all my Voodoos and I want you to come and see me do it.'

Carine had left her school not understanding anything of what was going on. But being the eldest of the five children, she knew it was important for her to go with her dad. 'We got to the church,' she said, 'and it was the first time I'd ever been in one. I didn't even know what a church was. But there were lots of people there, all of them singing and praying. They were full of joy. Then they burned all of my father's Voodoos. It was such a big celebration. But it was stressful for me too. I knew that people have died burning their Voodoos. But I could see my dad crying with joy. I'd never seen that before! Everyone was singing about the glory going to Jesus. I didn't know what that meant, but I'd never seen my dad like that before. I couldn't believe it. Then afterwards they took me back to school and later I told my mum, but she didn't believe me either.'

At that stage, the rest of the family hadn't heard what had happened to Alberic. Roland kept visiting with Alberic, and then Alberic began to meet with the pastor and the two of them read the Bible together. Alberic slowly began to understand more of what it meant to follow Jesus. Then, two months later, he tried to get in touch with Marhysa. Marhysa said she wouldn't speak to him, so instead, Alberic contacted a friend of hers. 'I've become a Christian,' he explained to Marhysa's friend, 'and I want to reconcile with Marhysa. I want to say sorry and fix things.'

Marhysa's friend passed the message on to Marhysa, but Grandma intercepted it. 'No way!' she said to Carine's mother. 'He'll end up killing you.'

'No,' said Marysa's friend. 'He's different. The way he talked to me was different.' She said to Carine's mum, 'Perhaps you should get together and have a chat and see what you think.' Eventually Marhysa agreed to see Alberic and a family meeting was arranged.

Hours later, Marhysa decided to forgive Alberic. They would get back together. They had never been divorced. But Grandma had one condition. 'If you're going to get back together, he has to live here with us, so I can keep an eye on him.'

In 1990, Alberic moved back in with Marhysa, Grandma and the family, under Grandma's watchful eye. The first thing Alberic did was to sit down with the family and explain to them that he was a Christian now. 'I've decided to follow Jesus,' he said, holding his

Bible and showing it to them, 'and this book guides my life from now on, so you will see me reading this and praying to God and going to church. And we won't be having any Voodoo anymore.'

All the family stared at him, not knowing what was going on. Marhysa said, 'Whatever you think.' She clearly didn't believe him. But at the same time, something had happened to her, just prior to Alberic's return, and it was changing her thinking. After years of believing in Mahu, and trying to be good, and thinking that being good would be enough to keep herself protected, Marhysa was starting to wonder. A Voodoo priest had come to their house and asked Grandma to become a witch. The priest said that if she didn't, a grandchild would be killed. Grandma said no, she didn't want to become a witch. Then the priest repeated his request, and his curse – that a grandchild would die. Grandma said no again and the priest went away. But a week later, Marhysa's small niece was eating her evening meal and she choked on a mouthful and died, in that instant. She was 2 years old. It was tragic. Grandma believed immediately that it was the curse from the priest, and Marhysa started to wonder as well. She knew it could also have coincidentally happened . . . these things do happen, but what if it was the curse? For the first time, Marhysa started to wonder whether being good enough was protection from the curses. She had always thought it was enough, but what if it wasn't? What if she needed a Voodoo after all, to protect herself and her children? The next day, Marhysa was about to call the priest to ask him to make them a Voodoo . . . and that's exactly when Alberic returned home, saying, 'No more Voodoo.'

'Are you sure?' said everyone.

'Yes,' said Alberic. 'I'm sure. We will have no more Voodoo in our house. It's true that the Voodoo has power, but the One I believe in has much more power. And because of his power, the Voodoo can't hurt you, or any of us, anymore.'

The next Sunday, Alberic announced that he was going to church, and he asked if anyone from the family would like to go with him. Marhysa said no. Carine's four younger brothers and sisters all said no as well. But Carine said yes. 'I just wanted to please my daddy,' she said, smiling. 'I was the eldest and I was always close to my daddy. I was the one he took out of school on the day he burned the Voodoos. And I loved him. So when he asked me if I wanted to go to church, I said yes, to please him.

'When we got to church, everyone was so kind to me. And Sunday school was amazing! I really enjoyed it. I wanted to go every week! So my dad and I kept going to church while the rest of the family stayed at home. On the third Sunday, a man asked if I would like to have a children's Bible. I said, "Yes, yes!" I was very happy. I started reading it with my daddy at home. I enjoyed it, but I didn't really understand it and I wasn't a Christian then. My heart wasn't touched yet.

'Not long after that, my mum started coming to church too. She loved it as well. She said she wanted to meet the One who had changed her husband. Of course, she knew he was completely different from the man he had been, and she wanted to know who could do this. She was right. He was so different. We all knew what he'd been like before – beating my mother and drinking. Then he changed. From that day on, he never drank alcohol again, and he never raised a finger for the next twenty years.

'He was completely different and we didn't know why. But I could see that he had so much joy in him, and that he loved my mum. Then my mum changed as well. She went to church and learned that she could never be good enough for God, but God loved her anyway; and that he had made her his child through Jesus. She believed in Jesus. She could talk to God! He wasn't distant,' Carine smiled.

'And guess what happened then?' she asked. I couldn't guess. I was still trying to write fast enough to keep up with her exciting story. Carine said her family were all back together again, and everyone was happy, and God was at work in their hearts. But then something happened that nobody was expecting. The man who had stolen the boat was found. It turned out that he was a man from Chile and he had previously been the boat's mechanic. He was charged and put in jail . . . and Alberic was given his job back. Alberic was even given compensation for all the years he had not been paid.

'All of a sudden my dad had a job and money again,' said Carine. 'But he kept saying to us that it wasn't the most important thing. He said he didn't really care whether he got the boat back or not. It didn't matter anymore. God allowed the boat to be stolen in order to bring him to Jesus, and that was the most important thing. That was amazing! My dad said if he hadn't lost the boat, he never would have believed in Jesus . . . and that somehow God uses everything that happens – good and bad – to bring us to himself. Quite soon after his conversion, my dad read the book of Job and he related to that story. He felt he had lost quite a lot as well, and he would often quote to us from Job 1:21: "Naked I came from my mother's womb, and naked I shall depart . . . may the name of the LORD be praised." He taught us to be thankful for what we had – that we had come naked and we will go naked.

'Then, one day, my dad held a public ceremony and he committed himself to my mum again. He told everyone that he was going to be the husband that God wanted him to be. My mum was crying that day. He was such a different man.

'For me, it took longer though,' said Carine. 'It took another three or four years until I became a Christian. I was just following along, going to church with my dad, because I loved him. Then when I was 13, my dad said that being a Christian was more than just going to church. I didn't know what he was talking about, but that year I went on a youth camp for ten days. It was a beautiful time, and on the last day of the camp, the youth pastor explained to us that we are all born sinful. We are all separate from God, on this side of the bridge, no matter who we are, or where we are. Sin puts a chasm between us and God, and we can't do anything about it; only Jesus can fill it – only his death on the cross can be the bridge to God.

'The youth pastor then told us to think about which side of the bridge we were on and whether we wanted to put our trust in Jesus that day. He said that if we did, we could stay in the room while everyone else left and went outside. I knew. I can still remember it. I was sweating all over. About five of us stayed in the room, out of 100. Someone came over to talk to me and we prayed together. I trusted in

Jesus and I immediately felt different. The weight was gone. I knew I was different. I wanted to call my dad straight away and tell him what had happened to me, so I did, and he was crying on the phone. He said he couldn't wait to see me.

'After I got back from camp, I told him everything and then I started going to Bible study at the church and I was baptised.'

I smiled with Carine. It was an amazing story. She told me more about her church and her friends and her Bible study, but I still wondered if the fear of her early years had gone away. Could she still hear the Voodoo spirits at night, after she became a Christian?

'Yes, I could still hear them,' said Carine. 'The Voodoo were still outside at night and we were under the same rules to stay inside. But I wasn't scared anymore. I was never scared after the day we burned the Voodoo with my dad. It is true what it says in 1 John 4: "the one who is in you is greater than the one who is in the world." Jesus is greater than any power! So the Voodoo spirits came to our house, because they liked to provoke the Christians, but they didn't have any power over us anymore. We weren't scared.

'My dad would go outside and tell them to stop. Other people would do that too, so there were some clashes in the town . . . because the Christians wanted to go outside and the Voodoo priests wouldn't let them. So some years ago, the government stepped in and now there are rules. If the Voodoo spirit is going to come out at night, the spirit has to tell the priest, and the priest has to give the people a warning – so they can plan when to go out and when to stay inside.'

We both thought that sounded reasonable, and I asked Carine what she had learned in her years as a Christian. 'I'm so thankful for my uncle Roland,' said Carine. 'He kept pushing my dad. He insisted that my dad go to church with him. And he went! So one day I sat down and I thanked my uncle for persisting with my dad, and my uncle said that he sensed it was time. Something was stirring in my dad. It made me see that deciding for someone else to follow Jesus is not our job. We just share the words that God has given us and he will do the rest.

'In our church in Benin now, people are being converted all the time. There are so many stories, so much energy! And so much excitement at what God is doing. Lots of people are seeking God and praying, and God is changing them, one by one. For me now, whenever I read about the fruits of the Spirit in Galatians 5, I think of my dad straight away. It says that beforehand the acts of the sinful nature are obvious (sexual immorality, idolatry, witchcraft, jealousy, selfish ambition, drunkenness, fits of rage) . . . "But the fruit of the Spirit is love, joy, peace, patience, kindness, goodness, faithfulness, gentleness and self-control. Against such things there is no law."[1] I've seen all of that in my dad! God does change every aspect of our lives, through his Spirit, for those who belong to Christ. I think to myself, I've seen it! I've seen it in my dad. I've seen God at work in him to change him, in all those areas . . . and that's been the biggest encouragement in my Christian life.' Carine paused, and she smiled her gorgeous smile. 'It's shown me, more than anything, that God cares for *each* of us. God loves the *nations*! God's story began with the nation of Israel, but he loves *all* of the nations, even Benin; he loves every single person, everywhere. It doesn't matter who we are or where we are, or the type of culture we've grown up in, even amongst the Voodoo. He loves us. That's what he did through Jesus, he loved the world! Because he loved my dad, and revealed himself to my dad, I got to know him as well. That's amazing!'

Carine explained that in 1999 she finished high school and she went on to study medicine at the University of Parakou, in central Benin. She graduated in 2009 and worked for some years in a hospital in Benin. During that time she met and married Yannick, and they moved to Australia in 2011. Sadly, when Carine was pregnant with their first child, her father had a stroke. Then not long after that, he had a second stroke. Carine spoke to her father on the phone regularly. 'The last conversation we had was a week before I gave birth to our daughter,' she said, sadly. 'My dad said to me, "Everything will be all right . . . God is in control." He said that very morning he had prayed for all of his children . . . but most especially he'd prayed for my child – the child who would soon be born – he prayed for her, that she would know the Lord, and that God would put his Word in her heart, very early in her life. Then my dad passed away that very night.'

Carine spoke sadly. It had been an awful grief. Her daughter arrived exactly a week later. 'At first I was angry,' she said. 'I wanted to know why. I wanted my dad to meet his grandchild – his *first* grandchild. He was only 68. It's not that old in Australia . . . although in Africa it's old. In Africa, if someone gets to 60 it's old . . . I cried and cried for my dad. It was so painful. I wanted him to see his granddaughter. It took me a long time before I could see that God's grace was enough for us and that, somehow, it was all still within his plan. That's what my dad would have said to me. He would have said that many things happen that are hard, but God is in control. I know that is true. My dad was ready to go . . . even that morning he told me he was ready to go. And then he said one more thing to me. He said, "Please tell people my story. Tell them what God has done in my life, and for me, and how he has changed my life. Please show them what God is like."

'That's what my dad wanted more than anything, at the end,' said Carine. 'You see, in Africa, people don't write. They don't write down their stories. They don't think of it. There are so many stories! There are lots of people in Africa who have had amazing stories, but they don't write them down and they all get forgotten in a few years. We forget what God has done! I think, more than anything, we should try and remember. We should try and tell the stories of what God has done in our lives.'

Carine paused and we both laughed together. I kept scribbling down her story, as fast as I could, trying to make a true record of the important, last words of Alberic, the boat captain in Benin, who became a child of God in the year 1989, and who, more than anything, wanted to tell the world what God had done throughout his surprising life. I'm sure he would have said at the end, 'May the name of the Lord be praised.'

13

I heard it three times

Joseph – Uganda

By October 2017 I knew I had one more story to go. At the same time, some friends of ours in the Blue Mountains had a visitor staying with them, and they said his name was Joseph. He had grown up in Uganda, and he lives there still. He used to be part of a strictly Islamic organisation. 'His story is amazing,' they said. 'You have to hear it.' So I did. I met Joseph one morning in the Blue Mountains.

We began with a cup of tea, and he told me that he grew up in the capital city of Kampala, in a wealthy and strictly Islamic family. His father worked in politics and all the family members were financial beneficiaries of Idi Amin in the 1970s. The family was large. Joseph's father had twenty-one wives and fifty-two children. In Uganda, it is legal for Muslims to marry up to four wives at a time, as long as the wives can be financially supported. Joseph's father was able to do that, and he also divorced them, one at a time, and married others. Joseph's mother was wife number nine.

Joseph then told me that, as a family, they were true believers of Allah. 'My family all went to the mosque every Friday,' he said, 'and they prayed five times a day – 7 a.m., 1 p.m., 4 p.m., 7 p.m. and 8 p.m. They strictly observed Ramadan each year, and they read the Quran in Arabic, every day. They thought it was the inspired word of Allah.'

'Did you grow up speaking Arabic?' I asked.

'Yes,' he said. 'I spoke three local languages as well as English and Arabic. I went to the local school. At the school, our teachers told us that it was our responsibility to contribute to the expansion of Islam, in any way we could. So I did! I was keen. I went to university and I did a teaching degree. After that, I worked for an Islamic organisation. We would spend our days on the busiest streets of Kampala, and we would evangelise Christians, and we would try to convert them to the Muslim faith.'

'Did it work?' I queried.

'Well, I would either talk with them one-on-one,' he replied, 'or I would help to run open-air meetings. At those meetings, the Muslim speakers would compare their Muslim beliefs with the Christian faith, and they would quote from the Quran and the Bible, in order to challenge the Christians. At other times, I was part of a group that went around disrupting Christian gatherings, or we set fire to churches . . . there was a big Christian meeting in 1988. There was an international evangelist preaching in a large arena in the city of Kampala, and I was with about twenty of my Muslim friends in the back part of the arena. We all had swords. We were ready to fight. I was the leader. Just then, the evangelist paused in his message and he said, "The Holy Spirit is telling me that there are people here who do not believe in the Lord Jesus." Then the evangelist lifted his hand and he pointed directly at the section where I was standing with my friends. "May the Lord bless them," he said, "and may they come to know Jesus."'

Joseph remembers being surprised – and then very quickly the police appeared behind him and his friends, and the whole group were arrested and put in prison. But the next day Joseph's father arrived at the prison. He bribed the police and Joseph was released. Joseph went straight back to his Islamic evangelism. It went on for years, until one particular day – Wednesday, 14 April 1993.

On that particular day, Joseph was 24 years old, and he had been up early, doing person-to-person evangelism on the busy streets of Kampala, until 9.15 a.m. At 9.15 a.m., he said, he began talking with a man who appeared to be doing the same thing. Except that the man was trying to convert Muslims to the Christian faith. After Joseph spoke to the man for about two minutes, he realised that the man had previously been a Muslim and he had converted to following Jesus.

'That's when I offered to pray for him,' said Joseph. 'I knew that bringing a person back to the Muslim faith is one of the greatest things I could do! So I spent hours talking with the man. We compared everything in the Quran and the Bible. I was sure I could convince him. We talked about so many things – Jesus and Muhammad, and going to church and the mosque. We debated about which was the true book of God . . . We knew all the verses. Then at 12.30 p.m., the man said he had to be going. He had a bus to catch. He asked me if I would like to give my life to the Lord Jesus. I said no! He said OK and he started to walk away. I watched him. When he had walked about 2 metres, I had a strange feeling in my heart – it was like a voice telling me that this man was taking something that belonged to me.

'So I checked my pocket,' said Joseph. 'I had my wallet. I had my keys. I looked over to where my car was parked and my car was still there. Nothing was missing. So I looked up and the man was still walking away. That's when I had the same feeling, for the second time. "This man is taking something that belongs to you." So I checked my pocket again. I had my keys, my wallet . . . It was all there. The man kept walking away. He didn't look back. Then I heard the message for the third time. "This man is taking something that belongs to you." So I went after the man and I told him what I had heard. The man said to me, "Jesus belongs to you. He died for you. He's welcoming you into his kingdom; he paid your penalty. But you have rejected him." I was confused. The man asked, "Would you like me to pray for you?" I said, "Yes!" I just knew in that moment that it was true.

'In our culture,' explained Joseph, 'when you surrender everything, you kneel, as a sign of submission. It's traditional. So the man said to me, "Would you like to kneel?" I looked around me. It was the heart of the city, at the busiest time of day. There were people walking everywhere. I said, "Fine." So I knelt down on the pavement on that busy street, and then he said to me, "Would you like to remove your hat?" I was wearing my Muslim hat, so I said, "Yes," and I took off my hat. Then he said to me, "Would you like to repeat these words after me – 'Jesus Christ, I need you. I thank you for dying on the cross for my sins. I ask you to forgive my stubbornness and my arguments. Today I confess with my mouth and believe in my heart that you are Lord, and I am saved, a born-again Christian. Please change my heart and make me the kind of person you would like me to be, Amen.'"

The man finished speaking and Joseph repeated the words after him. The man placed his hand on Joseph's head and he prayed for him. Then they parted. The man said that he lived in a village 64 kilometres away, and he needed to catch his bus.

'Did you ever see him again?' I asked.

'No,' replied Joseph.

'What were you thinking, as he walked away?'

'Afterwards, I questioned myself, a little bit. Did the words come from me, or from him? But all the time, in my heart, I was so sure. I was different. I knew. I felt peace at once.'

'What happened next?'

Joseph said that at that time, he had two wives and four small daughters. His house and property belonged to his father, who had given the house to Joseph while he was at university. Joseph went home that day and he told both his wives what had happened. He called them into the sitting room and told them that he had met a guy and decided to give his life to the Lord Jesus Christ. Immediately, the wives said they would tell his father.

Three days later, Joseph's father came over to visit. He was very angry. He sat down and said to Joseph, 'I have been told that you have deserted Islam and converted to Christianity. Is this true?'

Joseph said, 'Yes, I have done so.'

His father became even angrier. 'How could you do such a thing,' he asked, 'when you know for sure that Christianity is wrong and Islam is right? I invested my money in you! I sent you to university so that you could be a good servant of Islam! How could you do this to me?'

Straight away, Joseph's father said that he would take Joseph back to the mosque so that he could repent in front of the imam. But Joseph said no. He had already made his decision. Joseph's father became even more concerned. He tried to calm down. He began to counsel Joseph, and he asked him what changed his mind. Joseph explained that he had been speaking to someone, and that together they had compared the Bible and the Quran, and Jesus and Muhammad.

'It made me convinced,' said Joseph, 'that the two books cannot both be true. The Muslims believe that the Quran is the inspired revelation given to the prophet Muhammed. The Quran itself identifies three sets of books from the Bible that are also divine revelation given to trusted messengers. These three books include the *Towrat* (the five books given to Moses), the *Zabur* (the Psalms given to David), and the *Injil* (the Gospel given to Jesus). But those three books and the Quran contradict each other. The stories contradict each other.'

Joseph's father wanted to know more. 'Which stories?' he asked. Joseph explained that the Bible tells a story of Noah and his three sons who survived the flood. But the Quran says that one of Noah's sons died in the flood because he disobeyed Noah and refused to enter the ark. Also, the Bible tells a story about Abraham. Abraham was prepared to sacrifice his son Isaac. But the Quran says that Abraham was planning to sacrifice his son Ishmael. Then there was Moses. The Bible says that Moses was placed as a baby in a papyrus basket in the River Nile, and was later found by the Pharaoh's daughter. The Quran says that Moses was found by the Pharaoh's wife. Later in the Bible, in the book of Daniel, it says that three men were thrown into the furnace for refusing to worship the image of gold. But the Quran says that it was Abraham who was thrown into the furnace. More than all of that, the Bible says that Jesus is the Son of God, and the Quran says that he is not. The Bible says that Jesus was crucified on a cross. The Quran says that he was not crucified. It says that Jesus did not die, but that he was taken immediately to heaven.

'So these two books cannot both be true,' said Joseph. 'They contradict each other.'

'I agree,' said Joseph's father. 'But what makes you think that the Bible is more truthful than the Quran?'

'Well,' said Joseph, 'it's because the Quran mentions the Bible. It mentions the *Towrat*, the *Zabur*, and the *Injil*, so the Quran is a witness to the Bible. But the Bible does not mention the Quran. It does not say anything about another revelation to come. The stories in the Quran were taken out of the Bible. Therefore, the Bible is more truthful.'

At this point, Joseph's father demanded that Joseph leave his house. 'You can no longer be my son,' he said. 'I disown you.' Joseph's father then told Joseph's two wives and their four little daughters to get into his own car. They must go with him. According to local custom, Joseph's father had paid a dowry for both wives, so they actually belonged to Joseph's father, as did Joseph's four daughters. The wives and daughters got in the car. Joseph himself took a small bag of clothes and his documents, and he left. Joseph's father locked the door of the house with a padlock, and he also left, taking Joseph's family with him.

At this point in the story, I stared at Joseph, wondering how he felt, standing on the path, watching his family drive away.

'It was hard,' said Joseph. 'But I was so sure. I was convinced in my heart that Jesus was Lord. I had felt peace in my heart, when I prayed. I knew that Jesus was the only way to the Father. So what else could I do? I didn't want to cause a scene. I couldn't do anything, so I put my clothes in my car and drove to my mother's place. She lived about 10 kilometres away.'

When Joseph arrived at his mother's home, she had apparently already heard what had happened. People were talking about Joseph. They had seen the change in him, mainly because, in the preceding three days, Joseph had stopped going to the mosque, which he had previously done very regularly, and he had stopped praying five times a day to Allah. People had noticed the change in him, and they had passed the news on to his mother. When Joseph got out of the car, his mother saw him, and she did not welcome him.

'Is it true you have converted to Christianity?' she asked.

'Yes, it is true,' Joseph replied. 'My father has kicked me out of the house, and he has taken my wives and four daughters.'

'Well,' said his mother, 'I don't want to hear anything from you. You have brought shame on our family, and I am going to put a curse on you. In two months' time you will be dead.' Then Joseph's mother proceeded to put a curse on Joseph. She removed her blouse and she squeezed water from her breast. It was absolutely taboo in their culture. It was a terrible thing for both of them. The curse was consistent, though, with the very worst offence that a child can commit against a parent – to leave their Muslim faith.

Joseph said that he got back in his car and he went to a hotel. The next morning, he got up and dressed and went back to the busy street in the city where he had previously evangelised Christians. It was the same street where he had met the man, four days earlier. Now, on 18 April, Joseph started telling people, one by one, that Jesus loved them and that Jesus was the Son of God.

Joseph laughed at that point, describing it to me. 'I didn't even know how to preach,' he said. 'I didn't know very much. But I knew that Jesus was the Son of God and that Jesus loved them. That's all I knew. So that's what I told them.'

Then the rumours started in the street. The journalists came to find Joseph in the city, to get the story. Was this the same man who had been fighting the Christians for years, and was he really preaching Jesus? Wasn't he the defender of Islam? Wasn't his father one of the wealthiest men in the city? The resultant story made *The Uganda Times*. It was front-page news.

Joseph decided at that point that he needed to join a church. He went looking for a church nearby, but the first few visits didn't go very well. The pastors apparently didn't trust him. They knew who Joseph was – that he was the man who had spent years disrupting Christian meetings and burning churches – and if that was so, how could they believe his story? Had he really converted . . . or was he pretending, in order to join their church and cause trouble?

In response, Joseph decided to lay low. He kept to himself for two months, and he read the Bible by himself. He already owned a Bible because he had used it so frequently to challenge the Christians. But reading it now was different. Every page was speaking to his heart, he said. He began to pray. That was different too. Previously, he had prayed five times a day, as a Muslim. But now he prayed as a Christian.

'It felt different when I prayed,' explained Joseph. 'Previously, I prayed five times a day to Allah, but in between those five prayer times, I remained the same. I felt the same. But as a Christian when I prayed, I felt different. I felt encouraged and strengthened in my spirit as I prayed, and also in between praying. In Islam, I never felt different after praying.'

However, Joseph could not sit at home and pray all day. After two weeks in the hotel, his money ran out, and he had to leave and sleep in his car. After another two weeks in his car, he realised that he would need to get a paid job. Joseph had a degree in teaching but he had never worked as a teacher, having gone straight from university to serving with the Islamic organisation. As a Muslim evangelist, of course, he was very well funded by wealthy Muslims, who were keen for him to fight the Christians.

So then Joseph went looking for work as a teacher and, after a time, he found temporary, part-time work in two schools. He taught mathematics in one of them and physics in the other. After a few weeks, Joseph had enough money to rent a room. Then he discovered that, even while teaching at two schools, he had enough spare time to go back to the busy street and tell people about Jesus, which he did every day after school. One day, a Christian pastor came up to him and asked him where he was going to church. Joseph explained that he was not going anywhere, because the people didn't trust him. The pastor said, 'That's fine, you can come to my church.' Joseph did. He met other Christians and he grew in his faith.

'What's been the biggest change for you,' I asked, 'in becoming a Christian?'

'When I was a Muslim,' said Joseph, 'I believed that I had to do good things to gain favour. I deserved death, so I had to strive, and fast, and sacrifice, and work for Allah. I had to fight for Allah, and suffer for Allah, even in prison. That's all I knew. I believed that Christians were the enemy of Allah, so I must not love them. I must not be friends with them. I must hate them, and even kill them. I was never friends with them. But then when I became a Christian, I changed. I believed it was by the grace of God that I was saved. It was true that I did deserve death, but Jesus paid the penalty for me. He died for me. I valued what Jesus did for me and it helped me to understand the kindness of God.

'I began to understand that I can't do enough good things, but God loves me and I want to serve him because I love Jesus. Now, the difference is that I have friends who are Muslims. Before, as a Muslim, I would never associate with Christians. Now I am a Christian, and I have friends who are Muslims. Everything is different.'

Joseph continued his story. The following year, in 1994, he went to Bible school and gained a certificate in Christian ministry. Then in the next two years, he kept studying and he graduated with a diploma in ministry. But during those years, it was very hard. A large number of Muslims began targeting Joseph while he was doing open-air preaching. Other Christian preachers had been attacked or fled the country. Still others went everywhere with guards. As well as that, Joseph was also still teaching at the schools, to fund his study. His two wives and children remained with Joseph's father. After a time, Joseph's father apparently gave one of his wives to one of Joseph's brothers, and he gave the other wife to a driver. Very sadly, Joseph's brother developed HIV/AIDS, and he died, as did Joseph's wife.

At the same time, the threats from Muslim evangelists worsened. A Christian leader who was a friend of Joseph's had acid poured on his face by Muslims, and he became unrecognisable. About that time, too, a Bible college in Johannesburg, South Africa, heard about Joseph, and they offered him a place on their Bachelor of Ministry course. Joseph went, and he completed his study in the year 2000. Joseph then returned to Kampala and he was ordained as a pastor in one of the churches. In the same year he met and married his current wife, a local Christian Ugandan girl. Two years later Joseph became the senior pastor of the church and then, some years afterwards, he became the bishop of the whole area.

'What happened with the other members of your family,' I queried, 'especially your father?'

Joseph smiled. 'I didn't have any contact with my father for fourteen years,' he said. 'My father wouldn't speak to me. But then something happened in 2007. You will hardly believe it . . .'

In 2007 Joseph organised a medical team to come to Uganda. Fifty-two doctors and nurses flew in from Australia, the UK, the US and Canada. They arrived in Kampala and they planned to serve the health needs of the poorest people in Uganda. Joseph took the medical team to different districts in his country; the team ran health clinics and they gave out medicines. Every night the team members slept outside on the ground, and every day they treated the people free of charge.

One of the places to which Joseph took the team was a small village in the district of Masaka. It was 100 kilometres south-west of Kampala, and it happened to be the village where Joseph's father was now living, having moved there in his old age. Joseph, as he said, had had no contact with his father for fourteen years, and he knew that his father was still angry with him.

For four days the medical team worked in that village, a place that was only 1 kilometre from Joseph's father's home. Then the medical team left. Afterwards the villagers were thankful. They felt grateful for the care they had received and they were especially thankful to Joseph for organising the team to come to their village. They wanted to say thank you. When they realised that Joseph's father lived nearby, they went to his house, one by one, to say thank you. They said, 'Your son is a hero!' and 'His friends treated us for free!' and 'My teeth are fixed!' and 'I have medicines!' and 'Your son is good! He loves his people!'

The next week, Joseph's father sent for him. Joseph immediately travelled 100 kilometres to see his father. 'I had to see him,' he said. 'I didn't fully believe that he wanted to see me. I doubted. It had been fourteen years, but his message to me was, "Come, we have to talk." So I went. I told my driver to take me there straight away. When I got to my father's house, I went inside and we sat down, and he said that he was sorry. He said, "Thank you for the work you are doing – everyone is now happy." It seemed that even my father had received a pain medication that was working. Then he said one more thing. He said, "I thought you were wrong, but now I think you are right. I'm sorry."'

Joseph stayed with his father for three days. He shared his faith with him. The next year, in 2008, Joseph's father gave his life to the Lord Jesus.

'Wow,' I said. 'And the rest of your family?'

'In 2009 my father decided that, as a Christian, he should only have one wife. So he chose one, and he gave the others properties, which they accepted. Then my father's wife also gave her life to the Lord. After that, nine of my siblings became Christians.' Joseph smiled again. 'And it's not over yet.'

I nodded and agreed with him. 'Are you still working for the church?' I asked.

Joseph explained that in 2013 he was still on the preaching team of his church and the council of elders and, in combination with that, he took on an extra role working as a counsellor with an international peacemaking organisation. He began travelling to different parts of Africa where there had been wars and conflicts, particularly in Southern Sudan, and the Democratic Republic of the Congo. The rebels needed help in surrendering their arms, and the people in the camps needed counselling and help with reconciliation, prior to re-location. He said he immediately loved the work and is still involved with it. On occasions, he has also been detained while travelling in Arab countries, mainly because of his Muslim name, as recorded on his passport.

'My passport name is of Muslim origin,' he explained, 'but my records say that I am a bishop of the Christian church, so people get suspicious. It's been a regular challenge,' he admitted. 'But I love the Lord. Even when I am detained in other countries, I always see it as another opportunity to share my faith. And always, I know that God is with me.'

Joseph and his wife and four children now live in a 'green zone' in Kampala; they have to be very careful. They have a guard at their house, and the guard accompanies them to church, or any other travel, because there are people there who want to murder him. But Joseph is philosophical about it. 'We have to have a guard,' he says. 'That's how it is. But I love my country and I want to stay there.' He paused. 'You haven't asked me why I am visiting Australia.'

I smiled. 'Why are you visiting Australia?'

'Well, I was in Munich in 2003,' said Joseph, 'involved in an evangelistic work, and I was sitting on a park bench and a man came up to me. He was an Arab man from Iran. He assumed that I was a Muslim too, and he told me about Australia. He said that there were Muslims here planning to evangelise Australia, through Muslim men marrying Australian girls. As he talked to me, I immediately felt God asking me to go – to go to Australia and share the gospel with Australians. But back then I had no contacts in Australia, and I had no visa. So I said to God, "If you want me to go to Australia, please give me a sign, and a way to get there."

'The following month, when I was back in Kampala, I decided to travel to Nairobi to ask about a visa to Australia. I took my passport and I boarded a bus . . . I told the lady in the embassy in Nairobi that I wanted to go to Australia. She gave me the visa application and she said, "Who is inviting you to Australia?" She knew the rules, that everyone needs a letter of invitation to get a visa to Australia. I said to her, "I am a Christian." Then I asked her if I could talk to her privately, as there were people waiting in the queue. She said that she could meet me the following day, so we met . . . and her husband came as well.

'We talked together. It turned out that the woman was a Christian . . . and so was her husband. Then her husband said that his father was living in Australia; he could give me a letter of invitation, and he could pick me up from the airport. The next day, they organised all of that and they gave me the letter of invitation, inviting me to Australia, and they stamped my passport with a visa to Australia. So that's why I came to Australia the first time.' Joseph smiled. 'While I was here, I met people from a church in South Sydney, and they invited me back every year after that, to share the gospel with the people of Australia. I can't remember the number of people who have given their life to the Lord while I've been here in Australia, even last week.'

'What happened last week?' I asked.

'I was in Perth,' said Joseph, 'on my way to Sydney – in transit. I was sitting in the airport terminal and I saw a white man crying. I had never seen a white man crying before. So I asked the white man what was wrong. He said he wanted to kill himself because his girlfriend had left him. I listened to the man. I ministered to him. Then they announced my flight to Sydney. It was the final boarding call. But I was talking with the man, and he was still crying, so I didn't get up. I missed my flight to Sydney and we kept talking. I told the man about Jesus. Then I asked the man if he wanted to pray with me, and he did. He gave his life to the Lord, in the airport terminal.

'But then he said he didn't know what to do next. He told me that his house was full of charms and other New Age things and he needed help to get rid of them. So I asked the man if he knew any Christian pastors, and he didn't. So I left the airport terminal and I went with the man to his house and we got rid of the charms. We built a fire in the backyard and we burned the charms. Then we looked for the nearest church in his suburb. We rang the name of the nearest pastor; the pastor came over that afternoon, and he talked with us, and helped the man, and then the pastor drove me back to the airport, and I purchased another ticket for the next flight to Sydney. But before I left, the white man said to me, "Thank you. You saved my life."'

'Wow!' I said, trying to imagine the airport scene, and wondering if this was possibly a regular occurrence for Joseph.

'Everywhere I go,' he said, 'I want to tell people about Jesus. Jesus is the truth, the only way to the Father. You see . . . God loved the world so much that he gave his only Son, so that whoever believes in him will not die but have eternal life.[1] That's the truth and that's why I want to help the people in Australia to know Jesus.'

At that point in the story, I knew that we could have kept talking for hours because Joseph had an endless number of stories to recount, but I also knew that he had a train to catch. Catching a train in the

Blue Mountains isn't quite like catching a flight from Perth to Sydney, but it's still something. So I asked Joseph my final question. 'If you ever were to meet that man again,' I said, 'the one you spoke to on the streets of Kampala, on 14 April 1993 . . . what do you think you would say?'

'I would say "thank you,"' said Joseph, 'and "God bless you."'

I smiled, and also said thank you to Joseph, and 'God bless you' as we said goodbye at the train station. Then I turned to go home, partly wondering who Joseph might meet on the Blue Mountains train, and the conversations they might have, and the decisions they might come to . . . either over time, or on the spot, for the Lord Jesus. Then as I pictured those conversations, I was amazed again that God is at work every day, in airports and on trains and the busy streets around us, because he so dearly loves us, and because the story is not over yet.

Conclusion

When I initially began searching for the stories, I thought that I might find a pattern, or some general way that God tends to work as he draws people to himself, through his Son, the Lord Jesus . . . or perhaps I would find a common question that we all sit with, prior to understanding the gospel. Afterwards, of course, I realised that I didn't find a pattern. Instead, I found a God who is at work in the world, in ways completely beyond us. He loves his people, to the ends of the earth – in the flat, dry towns of Uganda, and the airport in Singapore, and the hospital in Alice Springs, and the Amazon jungle, and the bare hillside in the former Soviet Union, and the church in Benin, and the destroyed town of Penjwen, northern Iraq. He pursues each of us passionately. He wants us to know him, and he reveals himself to us in different ways, in different timeframes, whether we're looking for him, or not, whether we're desperately sad, or happily fitting in at the gym, whether we've run out of food, or making $100,000 a month. He knows us, he loves us, he wants us to know him . . . and he provides a way for us to know him, through the death and resurrection of his Son.

I didn't find a pattern, but I found lots of other interesting things – which is probably what you'd expect when you speak to such a variety of people from around the world! It struck me that regardless of our religious background or world view, many of us have some kind of sense that we're trying to be good. And we can't do it. Michael was trying to do enough good to outweigh the bad in Tehran. Judith felt that God had given her a 10-metre leash in Vienna, Austria, and that doing good things would lead to material rewards. Sara was trying to appease the Hindu gods in Karkineta, Nepal. Rudra was trying to avoid punishment. Neither of them felt any hope. Christy was trying to secure a better place in heaven. Hama feared punishment from Allah. Angelina was trying to be good by taking communion. Jamshed felt dirty on the inside. Carine needed protection from the Voodoo in Benin. Even Birgit prayed, just in case. But Michael was right. In the back of our minds, we do realise that we can never be good enough for a holy God. How could we decide how much good is good enough? Could it ever be enough? Inside, we know that we can't be enough, and that our biggest, deepest need is for forgiveness – to be clean on the inside – but we wonder how anyone could love us like that. Then we hear the message of God's love and redemption through his Son, the Lord Jesus. We hear that he sent his one and only Son for us, and he died and rose again for us, while we were still sinners, so that we could be forgiven and so that we could know him . . . and we can't quite believe it. Is it true? Is it possible?

Of all the stories that I heard, it was Michael's description of reading the Gospels for the first time that stayed with me. 'I just fell in love with Jesus,' he said. He read the Gospels and he saw that Jesus was someone who practised what he preached. Michael loved him. He had never seen or known anyone like Jesus before. For some of us who have been followers of Jesus for a long time, I think we need to remember that. The Bible is truth. It is full of life. It is God's Word to us today. It speaks richly to our hearts. It is the unbelievably compassionate message from God – our God who is unchangeable, sovereign, just, merciful, compassionate, and the only One who can heal, redeem and forgive us – and the One who says 'come'. In the words of the Bible we meet the Lord Jesus, and that's where we love him. Christy said that when she read the Bible, she devoured it, because Jesus was not like anyone she had ever met before. Sara read Matthew 11 and was amazed that Jesus could give her rest. Hama read Matthew 6 and he knew that it was true. Richard read Proverbs 3 and he knew that God would guide him, even through his blindness. Matluba put the *Injil* under her pillow because the words had given her peace. Angelina read the Gospel of John and she was amazed at the love of God. They wanted to read more. And so do we.

But as well as finding out about Jesus through the Bible, and loving him there, we are also drawn to him through his people. Almost everyone that I talked to described some moment of walking into a local church for the first time. Birgit was surprised that the people seemed happy. Chad noticed the camaraderie. Sara felt goosebumps and she couldn't stop crying. Judith said she was surrounded by people who were speaking a language she didn't understand, but they prayed for her. Alberic was welcomed. Cathy saw the leaders at Camp Howard and they cared for her. Hama noticed the different way that the Christians on the mountainside prayed. They were all impacted by someone who was friendly or honest or who showed kindness to them. Judith was amazed by the preacher who admitted that he had struggles in the Christian life. Alberic noticed that the pastor spoke directly to his heart. Judith was influenced by David Livingstone, who was passionately serving his community. Chad was drawn to Bruce, who listened to him, and who played music with him and who accepted him. Jamshed wanted to ask Adam more and more questions about Jesus. Richard asked his friend Cedric if he should become a Christian. He knew he could trust him. Over and over again, we notice that deep relationships – ones that allow us to share our faith, and to live it out with others – are profoundly important.

The other thing that I noticed, listening to the stories, was that there didn't seem to be any pattern in the timescale. Our journey to faith can be startlingly quick, like Joseph on the busy street in Kampala, or like Richard in the hospital, or Alberic in the church. But for many of us, it takes longer. We don't all hear the truths of the saving love of Jesus, in a clear way as children, or even as adults. We don't all respond immediately. But God is at work. He often gives us tiny glimpses along the way that stay with us. Somehow Judith knew that the cross and the light at Easter were very powerful. Somehow Matluba remembered the film about Noah. Somehow Hama heard the name of Jesus as a child and he wanted to know more. Somehow Christy prayed the "sinner's prayer" before she understood it. Somehow Angelina fell to the floor at age 40, desperately praying Psalm 104. Somehow Richard heard and remembered the gospel from when he was in Sunday school in Alekarenge.

God works in our hearts, over time, through his Holy Spirit, slowly revealing the truth of his gospel to us. Of course, after we come to faith in Jesus, the journey of growth and discipleship can take even longer! I really appreciated the honesty of Chad and Cathy and so many others, as they described the journey of faith that we are all still on. God is still at work! And we still have questions. Birgit would say, keep asking them. That's another interesting observation – often the questions we have early in life are part of what God uses later to lead us to the answer. Judith wanted to know about suffering. Michael wanted to know about the time before creation. Christy wanted to know about the reason she was here on the earth. Cathy felt like she was the wrong shape. Birgit feared the time when there would be no more of her. Chad wanted to fix everything himself. As we also spend time with our friends and family and loved ones, and as we truly listen to their questions, we may also find ourselves becoming a tiny part of their journey to find the answers.

That's the thing with the journey. We're all in the middle of it. We don't know what the future will hold, or how God will be at work. But we trust that he *is* at work today – within us, and around us. I loved seeing the impact of some of the stories on the people around them. Alberic's wife immediately noticed the difference in him, as did Carine and the rest of his family. They came to faith. Joseph's father said sorry to him fourteen years later. Some of Rudra's family became believers over time. But not all of them have made that decision. We're still in the middle of the story, and we don't know what God will do tomorrow. Michael's father is now listening to Christian radio in Iran, but he hasn't come to faith in Jesus yet. Christy is still praying for her mother. Jamshed and Matluba are still reading the *Injil* with their friends on the hillside and praying that God would speak to their hearts. Joseph is probably right now speaking to someone at an airport, or on a train station. The story is still going on, and we trust God for his timing and his plan. While we trust him, we know that we can pray. We can come to God wherever we are – when we don't have it all together, or figured out, and even when we feel shame. We can talk to him all the time, and we never need to show off, or pretend, or perform a ritual . . . because God is acutely, personally interested in our day-to-day. He passionately desires to be in relationship with us. He pursues us. He says 'come'. He is always with us. In the hard times, we hold on to that. We are never alone. The truth of that causes Matluba to dance on her bed; it causes Michael to keep going, when alone in Tehran; and it causes Richard to sit down amidst the red dust of Tennant Creek and quietly memorise Psalm 121.

The story isn't over and, because of that, we will continue to get out of bed and respond to God's love in whatever way we can, with everything we have, and often outrageously. Some of us might have an extra bag of *momos* to give away, or years to spend in Turkey, or time to retrain as a hospital chaplain, or the chance to serve in a Farsi-speaking church in the city, or the opportunity to bake cakes on a rocky hillside, or the gift of memorising Scripture using a MegaVoice, or a very big idea to use our extraordinary email network to create a new plan for discipling believers. Whatever you have, whatever you've been given, let God work in your life. That's what Richard would say . . . even when you think you've lost everything, or when you're no use to anyone, anymore. 'It's not over yet,' he would say. God is still at work, drawing people to himself, and making us more like him. So keep on living for the Lord. Allow him to work in your life, and he will.

And there will be a day when God himself will return, and he will completely renew his creation – the heavens and the earth. He will be with us, in all his glory, and we won't need the sun or the moon, because the glory of the Lord will be so bright . . . and there will be no more tears, or pain, or hospitals, or bullets in our walls. We will be made whole. And some of us may even run down the stairs.

Glossary

achar – spicy pickle eaten with *momos* in Nepal

Bahra Chuyegu – a coming of age ritual in Nepal where a girl marries the sun god

bael **fruit** – wood apple in Nepal

biaoboro – a form of cricket, Iran

blackfella – a term used of themselves by Australian aborigines

doko – a kind of basket

duomullah – a respected prayer leader in the Islamic faith

fulbin – a spiritist within the folk-Islamic faith

gargri – a vessel used to carry water in Nepal

goi – a disparaging term used by an observant Jew to refer to a Jew who is not religious

hijab – veil covering the head and chest area, traditionally worn by some Muslim women when in the presence of men who are not immediate members of their family

humpies – a small, traditional aboriginal shelter usually made of branches and bark with a standing tree as the main support

imam – Islamic leader

Injil – the Arabic name for the New Testament

jilli kurdi – traditional Kurdish dress, northern Iraq

jinns – bad spirits

Mami Wata – the mermaid Voodoo spirit from the sea, in Benin

momos – steamed dumplings filled with spicy meat, in Nepal

puja – the worship of Hindu gods or idols

raksi – local rice wine made in Nepali villages

salat – the second pillar of Islam – prayer five times per day

Santoshi Mata – the Hindu goddess, the mother of happiness

Satyanarayan – religious worship of the Hindu god Vishnu

Shani – the Hindu god of death

Sraddya – funeral rites within the Hindu religion

swag – a bundle of bedding used in Australia when sleeping outdoors

Swasthani – a Hindu tale recited during an annual festival in Nepal

thangkas – Buddhist religious paintings

time-payment – hire purchase

Towrat – the Arabic name for the first five books of the Old Testament

tupi – the traditional tuft of hair worn by Hindu boys in Nepal

Zabur – the Arabic name for the Psalms given to David

zakat – the third pillar of Islam – compulsory giving of money to the poor

Zi Char – a wide selection of affordable Singaporean dishes

zoolbia and *bamieh* – traditional Persian doughnuts, eaten during Ramadan

Notes

1 You are not alone

[1] Teaching English to Speakers of Other Languages.

2 What about the holocaust?

[1] James 1:13.
[2] 1 John 1:5.
[3] Psalm 23.

3 Why go back?

[1] 1 Timothy 6:7.

4 Who can bring change like that?

[1] Isaiah 52:12 (TLB).

5 It all came flooding back to me

[1] A massacre of indigenous Australians, one of the last events of the Australian Frontier Wars.

6 There would be no more of me

[1] Luke 8:10.

8 The wrong shape

[1] The Thorndale Foundation serves people with learning disabilities.
[2] See Revelation 3:20.

9 It was the way they prayed

[1] Although he didn't come to power till 1979, Saddam Hussein had been vice-president since 1968.
[2] Matthew 6:5–8.
[3] Matthew 6:3.

10 I was always curious

[1] See https://www.loyolapress.com/our-catholic-faith/prayer/traditional-catholic-prayers/prayers-every-catholic-should-know/prayer-to-the-holy-spirit (accessed 13 November 2017).
[2] Information courtesy of Wikipedia, https://www.wikipedia.org/.
[3] 1 Corinthians 11:26.

11 Clean on the inside

[1] John Robertshaw, *First Steps* (Cambridge, UK: Coastline Christian Resources, 1999).
[2] See Matthew 16:13–16.
[3] See Matthew 28:20.

12 More powerful than the Voodoo

[1] vv. 22–23 (NIV 1984).

13 I heard it three times

[1] See John 3:16.

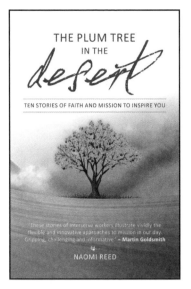

The Plum Tree in the Desert

Ten stories of faith and mission to inspire you

Naomi Reed

God is at work, even in the hardest places. From across Asia, the Middle East and North Africa, Naomi Reed has collected the stories of Interserve mission workers. These are stories of difficult situations in the mission field: some of victory and some that left the mission workers feeling they had failed. But despite the difficulties and perceived failures, each story speaks of the goodness of God and what it means to persevere and trust in him, even when it seems too hard. These stories give us a new perspective on those perceived failures and remind us that 'in all things God works for the good of those who love him'.

The Plum Tree in the Desert will build your faith and inspire you to action.

978-1-78078-141-9

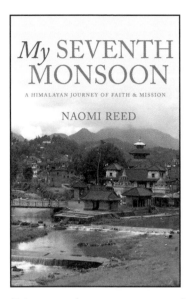

My Seventh Monsoon

A Himalayan Journey of Faith and Mission

Naomi Reed

'My seventh monsoon was the hardest of them all. I sat on the back porch of our Himalayan home and stared as the rain streamed down all around me. I had never felt so hemmed in – by the constant rain, by the effects of the civil war and by the demands of home-school. As I sat there and listened to the pounding on our tin roof, I wondered whether I would make it through. I wondered whether I could cope with another 120 days of rain. And in doing so, I began to long for another season . . .'

From the view point of her seventh monsoon, Naomi Reed takes time to look back on the seasons of her life. As she does so, she shares with us her journey of faith and mission and reveals poignant truths about God and the way he works his purposes in our lives through seasons.

978-1-86024-828-3

No Ordinary View

*A Season of Faith &
Mission in the
Himalayas*

Naomi Reed

'The Himalayan view from our back porch was normally breathtaking, but that day I sat there and wondered. Ten years of civil war, a deteriorating health system, an economic crisis and a political stalemate. It was a background of hopelessness for the lives of our Nepali friends and the community that we lived in. In such a setting of pain and darkness, how could God reveal his nature? And how could he call me by name? I wasn't sure. I didn't think it was possible.'

From within the uncertainty of Nepal's civil war, Naomi continues the story of her family's desire to train Nepali physiotherapists and share God's love in word and action. Her honesty and genuine longing to see God's purposes and sovereignty make this unforgettable reading.

978-1-86024-843-6

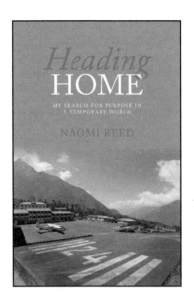

Heading Home

*My search for purpose in a
temporary world*

Naomi Reed

This is a book for anyone who has felt the pain of being in between homes or jobs or countries or roles or relationships. It's about our deep-seated human need to belong and enjoy purpose and community. After their six years in Nepal, Naomi Reed and her husband Darren and their three sons returned from Nepal to Australia and struggled with identity and disorientation. In this, Naomi's fifth book, she shares her story honestly and openly, allowing the narrative to lead the reader into prayer and reflection. By the end of it, you will feel a deeper and more profound understanding of what it means to belong to God and hope for heaven.

978-1-86024-853-5

Authentic

We trust you enjoyed reading this book from Authentic. If you want to be informed of any new titles from this author and other releases you can sign up to the Authentic newsletter by contacting us:

By post:
Authentic Media Limited
PO Box 6326
Bletchley
Milton Keynes
MK1 9GG

E-mail:
info@authenticmedia.co.uk

Follow us: